UK unemployment

Andrew Clark and Richard Layard

The University of Essex and the London School of
Economics and Political Science

*Pg→56
newspaper cuttings*

Second edition

Series Editor
Bryan Hurl
Head of Economics, Harrow School

Heinemann

Leeds Metropolitan University

17 0372854 2

Dedicated to the memory of Nigel Brown (1963 – 1992)

Heinemann Educational,
a division of Heinemann Publishers (Oxford) Ltd.
Halley Court, Jordan Hill, Oxford OX2 8EJ

OXFORD   LONDON   EDINBURGH
MADRID   ATHENS   BOLOGNA   PARIS
MELBOURNE   SYDNEY   AUCKLAND   SINGAPORE   TOKYO
IBADAN   NAIROBI   HARARE   GABORONE
PORTSMOUTH NH (USA)

© Andrew Clark and Richard Layard 1989, 1993

First published 1989
Second edition 1993

94 95 96 97 10 9 8 7 6 5 4 3 2

British Library Cataloguing in Publication Data

A catalogue record for this book is available from the British Library

ISBN 0 435 33023 3

Typeset and illustrated by Taurus Graphics, Kidlington, Oxon.
Printed in Great Britain by Athenæum Press, Newcastle upon Tyne

Acknowledgements

The authors would like to thank Bryan Hurl for much advice and encouragement. They are also extremely grateful to Marcus Rubin for all his work updating the tables and figures for this second edition.

The Publishers would like to thank the following for permission to reproduce copyright material:

Associated Examining Board for the questions on pp. 36, 49, 78 and 86; John Banham for the article on pp. 67–8; Steve Bell for the cartoon on p. 4; the *Daily Express* for the article on p. 1; the *Economist* for the articles on pp. 7, 32–3 and 83–4; the *Guardian* for the table on p. 58; Frank Hahn and Martin Weale for the article on p. 42–3; Mel Calman for the cartoon on p. 85; Richard Layard for the article on pp. 68–9; Northern Examinations and Assessment Board for the questions on pp. 36, 67, 78 and 86; Oxford and Cambridge Schools Examination Board for the questions on pp. 23, 60–1 and 86–7; Oxford and Cambridge and Cambridge Local Boards for the questions on pp. 23 and 86; Chris Riddell for the cartoon on p. 39; *Today* for the article on p. 56; University of Cambridge Local Examinations Syndicate for the questions on pp. 23, 66 and 78; University of Oxford Delegacy of Local Examinations for the questions on pp. 50, 66, 78 and 86; Welsh Joint Education Committee for the questions on pp. 49, 78–9 and 86; Richard Wilson for the cartoon on p. 89; University of London Examinations and Assessment Council for the questions on pp. 23–4, 36, 49 and 60.

The Publishers have made every effort to contact the correct copyright holders. However, if any material has been incorrectly acknowledged, the Publishers will be pleased to make the necessary arrangements at the earliest opportunity.

ii

Contents

Preface to second edition

During the so-called 'golden age of Keynesianism' which lasted for 25 years after the Second World War, unemployment, it was universally agreed, had been slain, if not by a sword, then certainly by the pen of J. M. Keynes. However, the spiralling inflation and spiralling unemployment of the 1970s and 80s respectively – caused by adverse shocks – themselves dealt a shock to standard macroeconomic theory as portrayed in conventional A-level texts.

For a while in the late 1980s unemployment fell, but it has been rising for practically the whole of the 1990s. Those who greeted sterling's 1992 devaluation and withdrawal from the ERM with enthusiasm see these as a trigger for changing the course of a recessionary economy and its endemic, monthly, gloomy rise in the number of jobless.

Andrew Clark and Richard Layard – in this rewritten and extended second edition – present the NAIRU concept in easily comprehended form, and they compare the 1980s recession with that of the 1990s. Read in conjunction with the two companion volumes in this series, *Deindustrialization* and *Supply Side Economics*, themselves both revised into new editions, it provides essential up-to-date theory and applied UK economics.

Bryan Hurl
Series Editor

INTRODUCTION

Complete idleness, even on an income, demoralizes'. Lord Beveridge

31 pits to shut ● 30,000 jobs axed ● £1 billion redundancy bill

MASSACRE OF THE MINERS

Britain's once-proud coal industry was last night brought to its knees by a savage programme of pit closures.

In one of the country's biggest industrial cutbacks,

31 collieries will be hit with the loss of 30,000 jobs – nearly three-quarters of the workforce.

Source: *Daily Express*, 14 October 1992

For many people, the loss of miners' jobs is only one symptom of the UK's recent poor unemployment performance. Unemployment in the United Kingdom is very high by historical standards. It is the major social problem of our time. Unemployment is a waste of our national resources, and this waste can never be recovered. Unemployment is thus inefficient: when there is so much work that needs doing and so many people wanting to do it, our society is clearly failing if it cannot bring the two together.

Further, as we will see in Chapter 1, unemployment is also unfair: not everyone in the economy suffers from it equally. In the UK, as in a number of other western economies, unemployment is concentrated on the young, the low-skilled, manual workers, and males. In addition, everyone in the economy suffers from unemployment because of

● the waste of the output that could be produced, as well as
● the tax payments that finance unemployment benefits.

Despite this, many people doubt whether anything like full employment is possible ever again. As in the 1930s, they consider high unemployment an act of God – the product of forces beyond our power to control. However, after the 1930s came the 1950s and 60s when unemployment was lower than in any previous period. Our present high unemployment is quite abnormal: it could be much lower.

Governments will not always act to reduce unemployment because they fear that doing so will spark off higher inflation. In Chapter 2 we present an economic model of the relation between unemployment and inflation.

In Chapters 3 and 4 we use this model to help explain the performance of the UK economy over the past twenty years, to describe how unemployment came to be as high as it is, and to dispel some myths about this rise.

In the last chapters of this book we use our model to propose some policies for reducing unemployment from its present high level without causing higher inflation, and we carefully consider a number of objections to these policies.

Chapter One

Some basic facts about unemployment

'Everybody needs to be needed, and for many people a job is an essential element in feeling needed.'. Charter for Jobs

Trends

Figure 1 shows UK unemployment rates since the last century. The many peaks and troughs indicate that this rate has changed often, and many times quite sharply, over the period indicated.

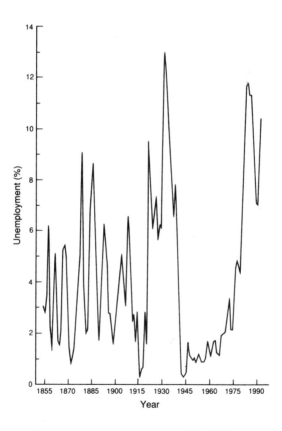

Figure 1 UK unemployment rates 1855-1992

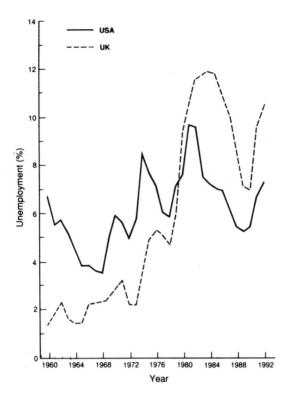

Figure 2 Unemployment rates for the UK and USA

Certain of these peaks and troughs can be identified as relating to well-known events. High unemployment rates in the late nineteenth century and in the 1930s reflect the Great Depression of 1873–96 and the deeper Depression of the 1930s respectively. Very low unemployment rates were observed in the periods of the first and second World Wars. Low unemployment rates continued on from the 1940s into the 1950s and the early 1960s. This was the time of the UK's long-lived post-war economic boom.

However, unemployment has risen in 17 of the 25 years since 1966. The average unemployment rate in the 25 years from 1942 to 1966 inclusive was 1.1 per cent; in contrast the average rate in the 25 years since 1966 has been 6.2 per cent. From 1966 to 1985 unemployment fell only in 1973 and 1979. The two big rises in unemployment occurred

3

between 1974 and 1976 and between 1980 and 1982 – after the first and second oil price **shocks** respectively. (In economic language a shock describes an unforeseen event which disturbs the economic system.) Unemployment fell from 1986 until 1990 but has since risen sharply again. The history of unemployment in the UK over the past 20 years is discussed further in Chapters 3 and 4.

Figure 2 shows the recent unemployment experience of the UK and US economies. The US experience contrasts with that of the UK: though unemployment has had an upward trend somewhat since the 1960s boom (associated with the Vietnam war), it is still now only a little higher than in the 1960s. Moreover, it fell sharply between 1982 and 1984, owing to expansionary government budgets, and continued to fall up to 1989, before rising again up to the time of writing. The recent rise in US unemployment has not been as dramatic as that in the UK. The performance of the US relative to the UK is an instructive one. Despite having a higher unemployment rate than the UK for much of the 1960s and 70s, the US has apparently avoided a steep upward trend in unemployment since the 1960s, and now has an unemployment rate substantially below that of the UK. The experience of the USA should remind us that no country is destined to remain typified by high rates of unemployment.

Definitions

What do we mean by an 'unemployed person'? The definition used in Figures 1 and 2 is based on the UK's **Labour Force Survey**. This is a survey of the population in private households in the UK, carried out on behalf of the Department of Employment. It has been designed to gather information on a wide range of characteristics of the population which are related to employment and unemployment. According to the survey people are counted as unemployed *if they are seeking work but do not have it. They must also be in a position to start work.*

This is a very natural definition of unemployment – a person has to be out of work *and* looking for work. The first part of this concept is very clear, because we can all see whether someone is not at work. However, the second concept is much more fuzzy, since there are many different levels of intensity with which people may seek work. The concept of 'seeking work' is especially unclear in relation to those married women who have not been working but now start to keep their eyes open in case a suitable job turns up. Thus the concept of male unemployment is more clearly defined than that of female unemployment. This is especially so for males aged 25 to 55 – nearly all of these who are not employed are unemployed (apart from 3 per cent, most of whom are invalids or students). It is therefore interesting to look separately at male unemployment (see Table 1). In terms of this the UK performs much less favourably with other countries than in terms of overall unemployment.

The figures we have given so far are based on the standard definition of unemployment. This differs from the so-called **official unemployment** or **claimant count figures** published each month in Britain, which are based on the *numbers of job-seekers getting unemployment benefits* (Unemployment Benefit or Income Support). These figures greatly understate female unemployment, for married women are not normally eligible for Income Support, nor for Unemployment Benefit if they opted out of making National Insurance contributions. Thus female unemployment in the UK, as measured by the official registered figures, does not correspond at all well to the standard definition of

Table 1 Unemployment rates by sex, 1991

	Males	Females	All
UK	9.1	7.2	8.3
France (1990)	6.7	12.1	9.0
Germany	5.0	6.3	5.5
Italy	7.1	16.7	10.8
Sweden	3.0	2.3	2.7
Japan	2.0	2.2	2.1
USA	6.9	6.3	6.6

Sources: UK, *Labour Force Survey* (Table 19, page 166, *Gazette,* April 1992); Other countries, OECD *Quarterly Labour Force Statistics* (national definitions).

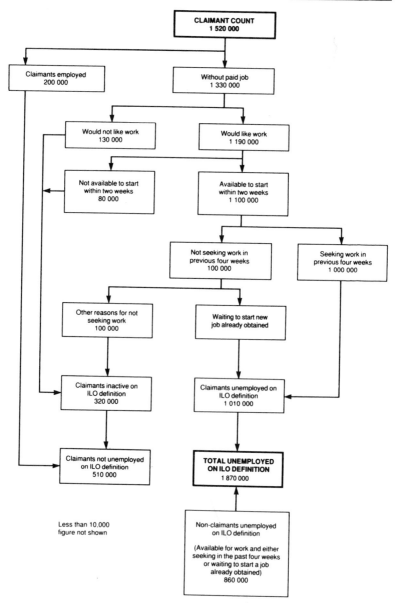

Figure 3 The monthly claimant count compared with the ILO measure of unemployment in Great Britain, spring 1990

unemployment. For example, in the spring of 1990 the Labour Force Survey measure of unemployment for women was nearly 400 000 higher than the official unemployment figure. In addition, from 1988 onwards it has been made progressively more difficult to get unemployment benefits. Whether or not this is a good thing, it sometimes means that the trend in the official unemployment figures exaggerates the fall in unemployment as measured by the Labour Force Survey.

Figure 3 shows how the Department of Employment reconciled the Labour Force Survey definition of unemployment (the ILO definition) with the official unemployment figures or 'claimant count' of those getting benefits.

The difference of 250 000 in the two figures is made up of several large counter-balancing numbers. The claimant count includes 200 000 people who are employed and 310 000 people who are 'economically inactive', giving a total of 510 000 to be deducted. However, there are 860 000 people who are unemployed on the Survey definition but who do not get benefits. Almost two-thirds of the non-claimant unemployed were women and about 60 per cent of these were married. This reinforces the point we made earlier about the accuracy of measures of female unemployment.

Counting the unemployed

A separate matter is how the official unemployed are counted. Frequent allegations of 'moving the goal posts' have been made by critics of the

---

Juggling jobs

How do you define a redefinition? On July 28th we said the Tory government has changed Britain's definition of unemployment 30 times since 1979; as it happens, all but one of these changes have reduced the official total. Not so, says Mr Robert Jackson, a minister at the Department of Employment. He insists there have been only two changes in the way unemployment is counted, plus another five changes in the rules that govern benefit-entitlement and thereby the number of people registering as unemployed – a total of seven amendments.

The figure of 30 came from the Unemployment Unit, an independent think tank. Mr Jackson, who has recently moved from the Department of Education, has produced a lower figure mainly by ignoring many changes in the benefit rules. But even the Department of Employment seems unable to make up its mind: as far back as 1986 its own monthly *Gazette* admitted to ten adjustments, some admittedly minor.

Since 1986 there have been two big changes: the introduction of the 'restart' programme (under which benefit-claimants are interviewed) and a tightening of the availability-for-work test. Together these changes have weeded out many who were previously included in the unemployed category. A study by the Bank of England concluded last year that this had reduced the official jobless count by some 750,000 – i.e. roughly half of the fall in unemployment over the previous three years.

True, many should not have been on the register at all; but the government can hardly claim the credit for cleaning up the statistics and for producing a 'record fall in unemployment' as well.

Source: *Economist,* 8 Sept. 1990

government whenever changes are brought in that reduce the government's estimate of unemployment.

The Unemployment Unit's Briefing 'Creative Counting' (December 1990) lists 30 changes to the way in which the official unemployment total has been computed since 1979 (the Department of Employment does not agree with this total – see the box 'Juggling jobs'). Some of these changes have had a large effect. For example, the decision in October 1982 to count only benefit claimants – as opposed to those registered at Jobcentres or Careers Offices – as unemployed is estimated to have removed between 170 and 190 thousand people from the count. More recently the provisions of the Social Security Act 1988 which deny benefit to almost all 16- and 17-year-olds have reduced the figure by almost 100 thousand.

The Unemployment Unit calculates unemployment figures using the definition that was in force in 1979. The estimates of unemployment shown in Table 2 indicate the extent to which changes in the definition since then have altered the figures.

Whether the changes to the count are a good thing or not is a separate issue. It is, however, important that comparisons of unemployment figures over time should use consistent definitions, otherwise differences due to counting technique could easily be allocated to changed labour market conditions.

By this stage you may be wondering whether the concept of unemployment means anything at all and whether we should be worried about it, since it seems to be difficult to measure. We feel emphatically that unemployment is important and that we should certainly worry about it. First, unemployment represents **economic inefficiency**. If in one year 10 per cent of the workforce is unemployed, then output will be about 10 per cent lower than it could have been (depending upon who the unemployed are). Further, unlike coal or iron ore, say, labour is lost for ever when it is unused; it cannot be stored and used later. Unemployment therefore represents an irretrievable waste of our national resources. Second, on **equity** grounds, unemployment reflects

Table 2 UK unemployment, September 1992

	Unemployment Unit estimates (1979 definition)	Department of Employment figures (current definition)
Seasonally adjusted	3 989 500 (13.6%)	2 843 300 (10.1%)

human suffering in terms of low income and low self-esteem.

Consider, first, income. In the 1930s the income levels on the 'dole' were much lower than today both in real terms and relative to income in work, so that it can be argued that suffering was greater then. Between countries, the incomes of the unemployed (relative to the employed) are lower in the USA than in Britain, but lower in Britain than in the rest of northern Europe.

As regards self-esteem, the effect of unemployment depends a great deal on how long a person has been unemployed. There is much evidence that people's morale sinks progressively as their unemployment lengthens. A person who has been unemployed for two years suffers far more each week than does one who has been unemployed for two weeks. So it is very important to know how long people have been unemployed.

How long does it last?

The answer in the UK is 'Depressingly long'. Currently, nearly half of all unemployed men have now been unemployed for over a year, and the 'average' unemployed man has been unemployed for about thirteen months.

Even more striking, much of the increase in unemployment has been via those who are experiencing **long-term unemployment** (out of work for over a year). This is shown in Figure 4. The number of long-term unemployed men rose from 100 000 in 1974 to about a million in 1986, and in mid-1992 it stood at over 900 000.

There is an important lesson in this rise in long-term unemployment. The number of people who become unemployed each year has risen relatively little. For example, the number of unemployed with less than two weeks' unemployment experience was the same in 1975 as in 1985, though total unemployment was up nearly three-fold. So if there has been no change in the number of people becoming unemployed, then why did unemployment rise so dramatically in the 1980s? The answer is that the people who are becoming unemployed are staying unemployed for much longer. The majority of people now, as earlier, are never unemployed, while those who do become unemployed now suffer far more than they used to.

To help us understand what is happening, let us apply a simple rule of thumb. This says that, when unemployment is constant, the number of people who are unemployed at any time equals the number who become unemployed each week times the average number of weeks they remain unemployed:

Unemployed = entrants per week × weeks unemployed.

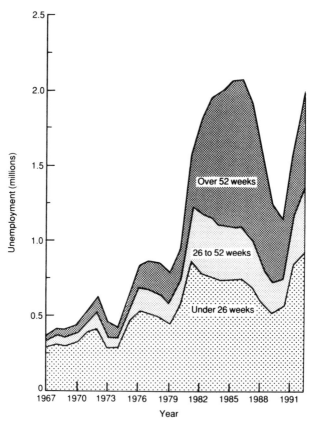

Figure 4 Male unemployment by duration

By analogy, the number of school students *equals* the number of first-year students *times* the length of the course. In the 'school of unemployment' the number of students has risen mainly not because of new entrants but because of a depressing increase in the length of the course.

Our formula makes it clear that 10 per cent unemployment could reflect two extreme cases (or anything in between):

● everyone becomes unemployed once a year, for on average 10 per cent of the year; or

● 10 per cent become unemployed each year, for on average a year.

It happens that the latter is far closer to the UK situation than the former.

As we shall see later on, this fact provides an important clue about how to reduce unemployment: we should concentrate on reducing long-term unemployment, and avoid trying to reduce the proportion of people who become unemployed. For this latter proportion is a powerful force restraining **wage inflation** (defined as the change in money wage levels over time), while long-term unemployment is not and therefore represents a total waste.

Given that long-term unemployment seems to be an important piece of the jigsaw, it is reasonable to ask why it is that it rose by such a large proportion when total unemployment rose. Might this even give us some ideas as to why unemployment has stayed high in the first place? Some suggestive evidence comes from comparing the durations of unemployment in different countries and relating this to their **social security systems** – that is the rules defining who can get what kinds of benefits and for how long. As Figure 5 shows, the length of time spent unemployed is very

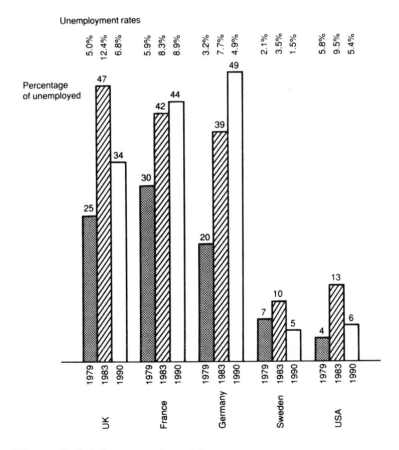

Figure 5 Adults unemployed for over a year

much shorter in Sweden and the USA than in the main European countries. Why is this? An obvious factor is the social security system. In the USA, Unemployment Insurance runs out after six months. After that the unemployed can in some states get a much reduced income on 'social assistance', but in many states a childless man who has been out of work for over six months gets nothing. In Sweden benefit lasts a maximum of 300 days. By then the person will normally have been offered a place on a training or work programme – and if he refuses that, he ceases to be eligible for benefit. By contrast, in Germany benefits continue indefinitely (though at a reduced rate after a year). In France they continue for nearly four years. In Britain, for somebody already on Income Support there is no reduction in income whatever as time goes on.

It is noticeable that countries which have open-ended social security not only have high long-term unemployment but have also experienced the largest rises in unemployment. This raises the question as to whether, when countries are subjected to a shock which depresses output and employment (such as the second oil price rise), they are more likely to develop a culture of unemployment if they have open-ended benefits. Such a benefit system may reduce incentives for the long-term unemployed to seek work, and may thus make it more difficult to reduce unemployment in Europe, unless specific measures are developed to deal with the problem of the long-term unemployed. In this context it is interesting to note that, as we write, there are moves afoot to reduce the duration of unemployment benefits in the UK, with the apparent intention of encouraging the unemployed to seek work.

How do people become unemployed?

In the discussion so far we have avoided any classification of the unemployed as *voluntary* or *involuntary*. Unemployment is, of course, affected by individual choices but by much else besides. However, it is reasonable to ask how individuals actually come to be unemployed.

The majority of unemployed men have either lost their job through redundancy, left their last job three or more years ago, or have never had a job. The proportion of unemployed men who had been dismissed rose markedly from 1979 to 1981 but has since fallen back to its earlier level. In addition, the proportion of unemployed men who had never worked before has been stable at about 10 per cent in each year. Among married women the proportion who were dismissed in the past three years or who had never had a full-time job is much smaller. More of them left their last job because of family, personal or health reasons, and it is likely that many of these are married women trying to get back to work after child-rearing. The detailed picture is in Table 3.

Table 3 How people came to be unemployed in the UK* %

	Men	Married women	Single women	All
Seeking first job	8	3	16	8
Left last job 3 or more years ago	32	32	30	32
Left job within 3 years, of which main reason for leaving was:				
Made redundant from regular job	22	13	12	18
Temporary job ended	10	7	10	9
Resigned from regular job	7	6	7	7
Family, personal or health reasons	7	27	14	13
Other	13	11	11	13

*The figures are rounded percentages from the spring of 1990.

Which occupations and age-groups are most affected?

It is time now to ask who the unemployed actually are: What are their skills? How old are they? Where do they live and in which industries did they used to work? The answer is that *the typical unemployed person is low-skilled, young, from the northern half of the UK, and with a background in manufacturing or construction.*

Skills

Let us start with the **skill mix**. In Britain in 1990, 72 per cent of unemployed men with a previous job were manual workers, half of them semi- or unskilled. The corresponding unemployment rates were:

Managerial and professional	2 per cent
All non-manual	3 per cent
All manual	6 per cent
General labourers	16 per cent

There is nothing new about these differentials, which incidentally reflect differences in the number of people becoming unemployed rather than how long they have been unemployed. In fact the ratio between the different unemployment rates has varied little over time. Ten or fifteen years ago, as now, professional and non-manual workers were much less likely to be unemployed than manual workers.

Age and unemployment

Another trait associated with different unemployment rates is age, as shown in Table 4. Unemployment rates are typically much higher for young people than for older people. Their higher unemployment rate arises entirely because they are more likely to become unemployed; but once unemployed they will remain so for a shorter period than older people.

High youth unemployment is due partly to the general economic situation and partly to the level of youth wages. Since the labour market went sour in the 1970s, job prospects have probably declined more for young people that for others, as firms have cut back on hiring. But since 1979 everyone aged 16 has been guaranteed a one-year place on what was the Youth Opportunities Programme, then became the Youth Training Scheme and is now **Youth Training**. School-leavers are put in training positions with work experience aimed at training them for a permanent job on completion of the placement. Entitlement to this scheme was extended to all 16–18 year olds, and since the autumn of 1988 all unemployed people of this age are required to accept a YT position or lose their benefit entitlement. As a result unemployment rates rose no faster from 1980 to 1985 for the young than for the middle-aged. From 1985 to 1988 the effect of the youth scheme was to cut unemployment rates for the young by more than the corresponding drop for the older age-groups.

The advent of compulsion for the under-18s to join the YT or lose their benefit (and so not appear on the official registered unemployment count) ensures that the unemployment rate of under 18s is extremely low. Table 4 shows that the unemployment rates for 18–19 year old men fell by rather more than the average for all men over the period 1985–92. This might be construed as evidence that the youth training schemes are helping 16–18 year olds find permanent jobs. However, Table 4 also

Table 4 Male unemployment rates by age, January

	Under 18	18–19	20–24	25–54	55–59	Total
1976	12	11	10	4	5	7
1980	10	11	9	6	6	7
1985	22	29	23	14	19	17
1992	1	20	20	11	12	13

Note that these percentage rates are not comparable over time, but do indicate the relative level of youth unemployment compared with other age-groups.

shows that the unemployment rate for 20–24 year old men fell by much less than average over the same period, which runs counter to such an argument. It seems that there is no conclusive evidence that the current youth training schemes are providing permanent jobs.

As regards pay, in Germany, where youth pay is relatively lower than in Britain, the youth unemployment rate is about the same as the adult unemployment rate. But in Britain there is evidence that between 1965 and 1975 increases in relative youth pay pushed up relative youth unemployment. Since 1977 the relative pay of youths has not risen and the rise in youth unemployment reflects the general economic situation.

As we have said, the typical unemployed worker is young. He certainly does not correspond to the common image of the unemployed married man with a large family claiming lots of benefit. In fact only 50 per cent of unemployed men are married, and only 24 per cent of them have two or more children. Thus most of them cannot possibly be (unkindly) described as social security scroungers with large families.

Industries and regions

We must now take a look at the industrial and regional aspects of unemployment, which are closely related. We can begin by examining the changing pattern of employees in employment (see Figure 6).

Since 1979 there has been an astounding collapse of manufacturing employment in Britain of two and a half million jobs – a much greater proportion than in any other major country. At the same time service employment has risen by less than two million (falling until 1982 and then rising). This change in the structure of employment largely represents the **deindustrialization** that mature economies experience where concentration switches from industry towards services. So total employees in employment fell by over one million from June 1979 to December 1991, though this was offset by a roughly equal rise in self-employment. Given the masculinity of manufacturing it is not surprising that male employment has fallen, while female employment has improved over the period.

The fall in manufacturing employment has hurt some areas more than others, especially the West Midlands and the North of England. Thus unemployment has risen more (in terms of percentage points) in the areas which already had high unemployment.

In Figure 7 we can see some of the differences in unemployment rates between different regions. Unemployment is not evenly spread across the country. These figures, of course, conceal immense variations within regions, where some towns have become industrial deserts. There are still whole streets in the North of England (let alone

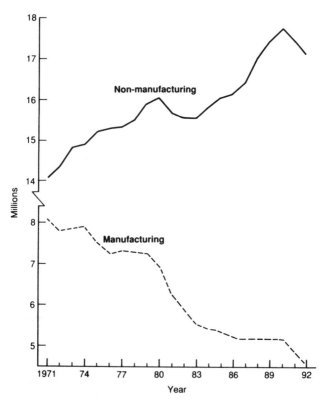

Figure 6 Employees in employment in the UK

Northern Ireland) where most people are out of work. But, taking quite large travel-to-work areas and using the official registered unemployment figures, here are some horror stories: Londonderry 20 per cent, South Tyneside 18 per cent, Rotherham 15 per cent, Liverpool 15 per cent, Hartlepool 16 per cent. By contrast the South of England can offer Crawley, Cambridge and Basingstoke, all at around 5 per cent.

The recession of 1990–92 differed from that of the early 1980s in that it hit the South East relatively hard. The result has been that over the past two or three years the differences in regional unemployment rates have narrowed noticeably from their levels in the late 1980s. This is discussed further in Chapter 4.

The industrial structure of unemployment (as opposed to employment) is not that clear a concept, since only 33 per cent of unemployed workers go back to the industry they were in. But if we classify the unemployed by the last job they had, then the situation in the early 1980s was as shown in Figure 8. Clearly, some industries are always

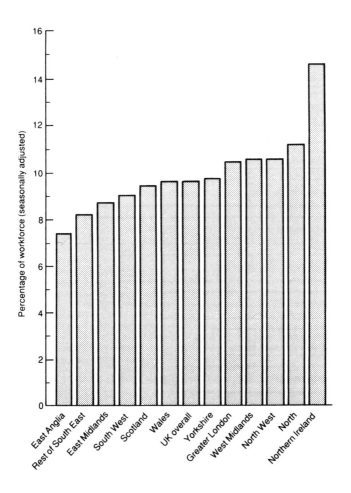

Figure 7 Unemployment rates by region, June 1992

more unemployment-prone than others owing to the nature of the work that they offer. One obvious case from Figure 8 is construction, where building projects are often short-lived and workers are unemployed for a while in between projects. (This is another case where the differences in unemployment rates are mainly explained by differences in entry rates rather than duration.) Even so, the fall in employment in the 1980s hit manufacturing and construction very hard, and manufacturing and construction are still the industries with the highest unemployment rates.

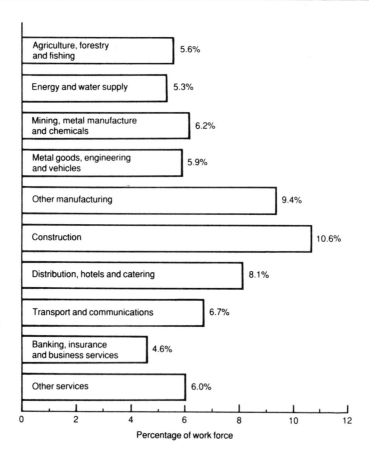

Figure 8 Unemployment by industry, 1990 (Labour Force Survey)

Unemployment and vacancies

Like any other market, the labour market has buyers and sellers. Up to now we have concentrated on the sellers – the employed and the unemployed – but we shall now look at the behaviour of the demanders of labour too. In the same way that the unemployed can be regarded as frustrated retailers of labour, then firms with **vacancies** can be seen as frustrated purchasers of labour.

Vacancies are advertised in a wide number of ways: at Jobcentres, by private employment agencies, in newspapers, on vacancy boards, by word of mouth, and so on. It is then rather difficult to be precise about exactly how many vacancies exist at any one time.

For any year we have reliable information about the number of vacancies that are advertised at Jobcentres, and we can use this to estimate a figure for total vacancies. In mid-1992 it was estimated that:

- there were 300 000 vacancies in the UK, a fall of over 50 per cent compared with the same figure in 1988;
- the South East has suffered disproportionately, with vacancies down two-thirds from their 1988 level;
- in the Greater London area on its own there are now an estimated 24 000 vacancies, compared with 96 000 in 1988.

Figure 9 shows the behaviour of unemployment and vacancies since 1956 by plotting one against the other in a 'U/V curve'. Both unemployment and vacancies are expressed as rates: unemployment is divided by the labour force (the sum of the people in work and the unemployed), while vacancies are divided by employees in employment. The 1950s and 60s were associated with low levels of unemployment and high vacancy rates, reflecting the tight labour market that existed in this period. The two oil shocks of 1973 and 1979 both pushed the curve in a south-easterly direction where there are fewer vacancies and more unemployment. The late 1980s saw something of a recovery in unem-

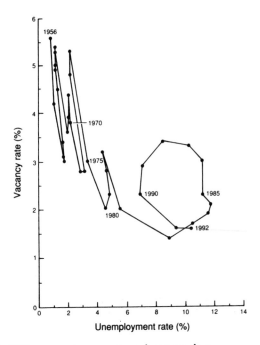

Figure 9 UK unemployment and vacancies

ployment, associated with the 'Lawson boom'. However, the experience of recent years has been depressingly similar to that of 1980-82, the worst years of the recession during that decade, and the ratio of unemployment to vacancies is still very high compared with those that prevailed before 1973.

Despite this high ratio, 300 000 empty posts seem like a lot when there are nearly three million unemployed. The existence of frustrated supply and demand together suggests that there is a degree of **mismatch** between the vacant jobs and the unemployed.

For example, suppose that workers could be split into just two types, the skilled and unskilled. Assume there are 200 people unemployed and 100 vacancies. Then it is possible to describe two cases, as illustrated in Figure 10. In the top panel there is perfect match, with the ratio of skilled to unskilled being exactly the same for both unemployment and vacancies. In the bottom panel, however, there is imperfect match, or mismatch, in that skilled workers account for only 20 per cent of the unemployed but 80 per cent of the vacancies.

Mismatch can occur for reasons other than skill. It is often said that the discrepancies between regional unemployment rates indicate mismatch, and that the situation is made worse by the difficulty of finding housing in the better-off regions. Mismatch may also result from a

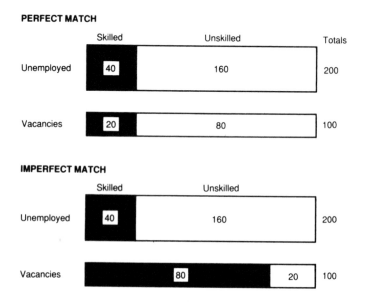

Figure 10 Mismatch (see the text)

switch of demand from one industry to another – unemployment would then result in the declining sectors until workers could redeploy themselves into the sectors that are now expanding. This type of mismatch is obviously similar to structural unemployment.

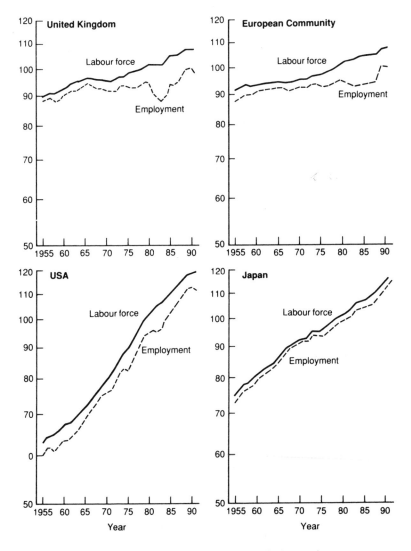

Figure 11 Labour force, employment and unemployment (plotted on a vertical log scale indexed to 1979 = 100)

The labour force and unemployment

Finally, there is an obvious question. Can the level of unemployment be explained by the size of the **labour force**? As a matter of arithmetic we know that

Unemployment = labour force – employment.

So if the labour force was lower and employment the same, unemployment would be reduced. In a later chapter we shall argue that over a longish run unemployment is not going to be affected by the labour force, since if the labour force rises, employment will rise. That has certainly been the case for most of the past 200 years. But at this stage let us just look at the facts.

In the UK the labour force grew substantially from 1950 to 1966 (see Figure 11) and unemployment was pretty well stable. The labour force then fell for the next five years before resuming its previous growth rate (except between 1980 and 1983). For most of this period since 1966 (of both falling and rising labour force), unemployment rose.

The contrast with the USA and Japan is striking. In both of these countries the labour force rose much more than in the UK (or Europe); yet unemployment rose much less. We can easily see this by comparing the slopes of the lines in Figure 11.

So why did unemployment rise so much here? In the next chapter it will be time to make a systematic attempt to find out.

KEY WORDS

Shocks
Labour Force Survey
Official unemployment
  figures
Claimant count figures
Economic inefficiency
Equity
Long-term unemployment
Wage inflation

Social security systems
Redundancy
Skill mix
Age
Youth Training
Deindustrialization
Vacancies
Mismatch
Labour force

Reading list

Armstrong, H., and Taylor, J., *Regional Economics*, Heinemann Educational, 1990.
Bazen, S., and Thirlwall, A.P., Chapter 3 in *Deindustrialization*, 2nd

edn, Heinemann Educational, 1992.

Ison, S., 'Characteristics of unemployment', *British Economy Survey*, Longman, autumn 1991.

Paisley, R., and Quillfeldt, J., Exercises 15 and 24 in *Economics Investigated*, vol. 2, Collins Educational, 1992.

Essay topics

1. Why are there regional variations in unemployment rates in the UK? To what extent would regional differences in pay reduce the divergences in unemployment rates? (University of Cambridge Local Examinations Syndicate, 1990)
2. 'Current regional policy offers no solution to the growing problem of long-term unemployment.' Discuss. (Oxford and Cambridge Schools Examination Board, 1992)
3. Analyse the main trends in employment in UK manufacturing industry since 1960. Discuss the main causes of these changes. (Combined boards of Oxford and Cambridge, Cambridge Local, A/S level 1990)
4. Analyse the factors which have led to the deindustrialization of the UK economy since 1970. Discuss whether the completion of a Single European Market will accelerate deindustrialization. (Combined boards of Oxford and Cambridge, Cambridge Local, A/S level 1991)

Data Response Question 1

The workforce and working practices

This task is based on a question set by the University of London Examinations and Assessment Council in 1992. Study Figures A and B and Table A and answer the questions.

1 (i) What is the difference between the terms 'working population' and 'the population of working age'? (ii) With reference to Figure A and Table A, calculate both the working population and the population of working age for 1988.
2 (i) With reference to Table A, how did the size and composition of the working population change between 1978 and 1988? (ii) Examine the factors that might have caused these changes.
3 (i) With reference to Figure A, identify the projected changes in the age structure of the population of working age between 1988 and 2000. (ii) Examine the likely economic consequences of such changes.
4 With reference to Figure B, discuss the likely reasons why some companies were altering their employment, training and working practices to increase the labour supply.

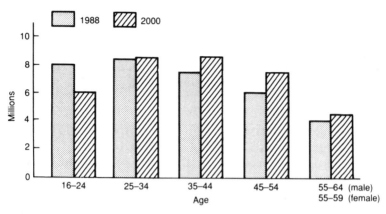

Figure A Estimates and projections of the population of working age

Figure B Percentage of employers altering their employment, training and working practices.

Table A The UK's workforce and population

	1978	*1983*	*1988*
Population (millions)	56.2	56.3	57.1
Total employees in employment (June) (thousands)	22 789	21 067	22 568
of which men	13 398	11 940	12 234
women	9 391	9 127	10 334
Wholly unemployed (June) (thousands)	1 343	2 984	2 341
Vacancies (annual average) (thousands)	210	137	248

Chapter Two

The causes of unemployment

'If the Treasury were to fill old bottles with bank notes, bury them at suitable depths in disused coal-mines, which are then filled up to the surface with town rubbish, and leave it to private enterprise to dig the notes up again, there need be no more unemployment.' J. M. Keynes

What has gone wrong? Governments do not like unemployment and it is not good for their re-election prospects. So why do they not reduce it? The answer of course is that they also dislike **inflation** and so do their electorates.

The only reason we have unemployment is that governments are using it to contain inflation. Generally, governments will not admit this. But if you suggest doing more to expand the economy, their answer will always be, 'That's inflationary'. In fact why else would they not do something desirable like creating jobs? Clearly, they *are* using unemployment to control inflation.

Thus, to understand unemployment, we need to understand the relationship between unemployment and inflation, and what affects it.

Inflation and unemployment

If unemployment is low, inflation will tend to rise. Employers will find it more difficult to fill their vacancies. So they will try to attract workers by paying more than the going rate. At the same time unions will feel in a stronger position to push for wage increases. But, if unemployment is high enough, inflation will be stable; and, if it is even higher, inflation will actually fall, as happened in the early 1980s and from 1990 to the date of writing.

Thus there is a critical level of unemployment at which inflation will be just stable – neither rising nor falling. We shall call this the NAIRU (the **non-accelerating inflation rate of unemployment**) – a terrible phrase but one that is preferable to its synonym: natural rate of unemployment. This is charted in Figure 12. *If unemployment is pushed below the NAIRU, inflation increases; and if unemployment is pushed above this point, inflation can be reduced.* The relationship between the change in inflation and the level of unemployment is shown by the sloping line. In the example chosen, the NAIRU is 10 per cent unemployment

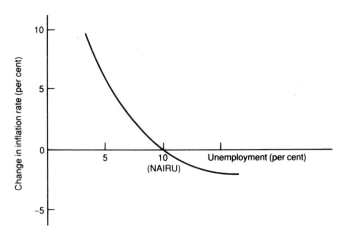

Figure 12 Unemployment and inflation (how inflation will rise if unemployment is below the NAIRU, and vise versa)

(or 2.8 million), which may not be too far from the mark. Starting from the NAIRU, a 1 per cent lower level of unemployment would make inflation rise by about 1 per cent a year – again a reasonably plausible estimate.

One might ask why low unemployment leads to rising inflation, rather than simply to rising prices. In other words why, when unemployment is low, do we find *inflation* rising, rather than *prices* rising at a steady rate of inflation? The answer is that inflation has a momentum (or inertia) of its own. If there is no particular pressure in the labour market, people expect inflation to continue at its former level. So if prices are already rising they will continue to rise. Extra pressure in the labour market will make them rise faster. Economic agents then apply **adaptive expectations** to their decision-making; trade unions, for example, recalibrate upwards their wage demands expecting the higher level of inflation to continue.

To see how reasonable this whole argument is, Figure 13 shows the history of inflation relative to unemployment. The panel (a) shows the inflation rate. The panel (b) shows the unemployment rate adjusted for the estimated change in the NAIRU. It is shown on an inverted scale, so that peaks on the graph reflect peaks in economic activity. It is these peaks which cause inflation to increase, while troughs cause it to decrease.

Thus the final panel (c) plots together the unemployment peaks and troughs *and* the changes in inflation. This last graph provides a potted history of the last 30 years. As can be seen, inflation tended to rise in the booms of 1956, 1961, 1965 and 1970 (all of them related to elections!). In the slacker intervening periods, inflation tended to fall (or rise less). The boom of 1973, however, had an altogether disproportionate effect on inflation. This was because it coincided with booms in most other countries, leading to an explosion of **commodity prices** (such as copper, cotton, rice, wheat and zinc) and the accompanying first oil price rise. Matters were made much worse by the **indexation** arrangements, whereby wages were increased in accordance with movements in the Retail Price Index, as prescribed by the prevailing

13 (a) Inflation

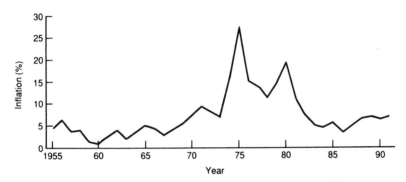

13 (b) Unemployment

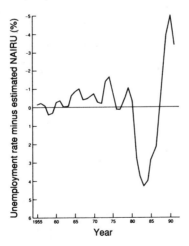

Figure 13 (a) Inflation (the annual change in the GDP deflator), (b) unemployment (deviation from estimated NAIRU)

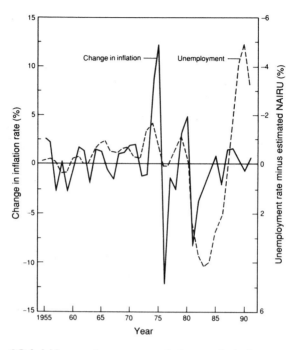

Figure 13 (c) Unemployment and change in inflation 1955–91

incomes policy. The passive policies of the incoming Labour government did nothing to dampen the fires of inflation, and by 1976 the situation was so critical that a drastic incomes policy (£6 a week for all, or 10 per cent for the average person) was introduced. This had a sensational effect in reducing inflation from 27 per cent in 1975 to 14 per cent the following year. The next inflationary surge came in 1979–80, following on the partial economic recovery of 1978–79 and the abandonment of the incomes policy. However this time the fire was put out by a huge dose of unemployment. This brought inflation down rapidly in 1981, and it remained low for much of the rest of the decade. It did not, however, fall as much as one might have expected, and we discuss the reasons for this in the next chapter, when we consider the recent experience of the UK. With the 'Lawson boom' of the late 1980s there was a marked fall in unemployment, accompanied by a persistent upwards creep in inflation. This advance in inflation continued into the early 1990s until it was punctured by the deflation of the 'Lamont bust'.

Thus there is a clear relationship between unemployment and inflation, but only if we recognize the fact that the NAIRU has risen.

We can summarize the lessons so far in terms of Figure 14. If unemployment is at the NAIRU, inflation is stable; but if more people are employed, inflation will tend to rise. The curve is the modern version of the so-called **Phillips curve**. The NAIRU is sometimes called the '*natural' rate of unemployment*, but this is misleading because it seems to imply that it is inevitable. In fact, however, a major objective of policy is to reduce it.

In the long run (when inflation *has* to be stable) unemployment will settle down at the NAIRU. But in the short-term unemployment depends on the growth of aggregate money spending (or aggregate demand) relative to the inflation rate. Thus suppose that in Figure 14 we were at the NAIRU last year and inflation was 5 per cent. This year money spending rose by 10 per cent. The result, as illustrated at point P in the figure, is a rise in inflation *and* a rise in employment. The split between extra inflation and extra employment depends on the slope of the Phillips curve (and on productivity growth). *But a rise in the growth rate of money spending will always increase inflation and employment, compared with what they would otherwise be. The reverse is also true.*

Thus, in the short term, employment and inflation are jointly determined by aggregate *money* demand and the aggregate supply behaviour summarized in the Phillips curve. The resulting level of output is generally called **real aggregate demand.**

Figure 14 implies that government policy to reduce unemployment below the NAIRU will only work in the short run unless the NAIRU itself can be changed; and even this short-run reduction in unemploy-

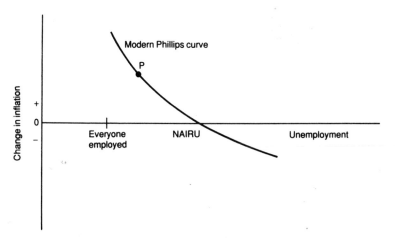

Figure 14 Application of the modern Phillips curve

In all candour

In 1976, Mr James Callaghan, the Labour Prime Minister, launched a celebrated attack on the previous Keynesian orthodoxy which had recommended policies to raise employment whenever this was judged to be less than 'full', whatever the inflationary consequences. He said:

'We used to think that you could spend your way out of a recession and increase employment by cutting taxes and boosting government spending. I tell you in all candour that the option no longer exists, and that insofar as it ever did exist, it only worked on each occasion since the war by injecting a bigger dose of inflation into the economy, followed by a higher level of unemployment as the next step. Higher inflation followed by higher unemployment. We have just escaped from the highest rate of inflation this country has known; we have not yet escaped from the consequences: high unemployment. That is the history of the last twenty years'.

---

ment will come at the expense of rising inflation. Consider again a change in government spending that moves the economy from the NAIRU to point P. In the short run unemployment falls (for example from 10 to 7 per cent) and inflation accelerates, say from 5 to 10 per cent. In the long run the economy will be back at the NAIRU (i.e. with unemployment of 10 per cent again), but the rate of inflation will now be 10 per cent instead of the initial 5 per cent (remember that the vertical axis of Figure 14 measures the *change* in inflation, not the *level* of inflation). *Therefore government policy can reduce unemployment for a short period without changing the NAIRU, but only at the price of a permanently higher rate of inflation.*

The rise in unemployment

We can now come back to unemployment, and think of its rise as consisting of two parts:

- First, there is the rise in the NAIRU, which needs to be explained in detail.
- Second, there is an 'overkill' – a rise in unemployment above the NAIRU, resulting in a fall in inflation; or there is an 'underkill' – a fall in unemployment below the NAIRU, resulting in a rise in inflation.

The overkill or underkill

Let us start with the **overkill,** sometimes called Keynesian unemployment. In the short run the level of unemployment is determined by 'real aggregate demand', that is, by the demand for British output. In the early 1980s this demand fell sharply relative to our potential output, much of this fall resulting from government policy. The fall in demand raised unemployment by at least five percentage points. High priority was given to *reducing* inflation by reducing demand. From our discussion of Figure 12 it is obvious that a policy of reducing inflation will involve a rate of unemployment higher than the NAIRU – the overkill.

In a position where inflation is falling, there are two ways to ameliorate the unemployment position. The quickest is to raise employment by spending more money now, and accept that when the NAIRU is reached inflation will still be at the present level. The alternative is not to boost money spending, but to rely on falling inflation to increase the real value of this spending. This takes much longer, but it also works. It is even possible that eventually, as in the late 1980s, there may be a danger of **underkill** as real spending recovers. At this point, there will be signs of upward pressure on inflation – or, in the language of science, of **overheating** – as the growth in demand outstrips the ability of the economy to supply goods without a rise in prices.

Factors affecting the NAIRU

So much for the 'demand side' factors affecting unemployment. But there is also the rise in the NAIRU, which has reduced the ability of the economy to supply extra output without this leading to extra inflation. This is what people mean when they talk about the importance of improving the **supply side** of the economy. By this term they do not simply mean improving the supply of labour; they mean everything which affects the ability of the economy to provide a sustained supply of output at stable inflation.

So what factors may have increased the NAIRU? There are a whole host of possible explanations, including:

- the two oil price rises of 1973 and 1979;
- the slowdown in productivity growth;
- the rise in taxation;
- easier access to social security benefits;
- more mismatch between jobs available and the qualities of the unemployed;
- employment protection (making it harder to sack workers once hired);
- increases in union militancy;
- the likelihood that high unemployment in the recent past can raise the NAIRU, at least temporarily.

All or any of these factors could have played a role, and we shall discuss some of the more salient ones in the next chapter. But, before we can do this, we need some general idea about how the NAIRU is determined. We can then use this framework to look at the factors which must affect it.

How the NAIRU is determined

The theory is very simple. In a nutshell, there is at any particular time a limit to the living standards which the economy can provide to its workers. In other words there is a **'feasible' real wage** (the money wage divided by the price index). If workers try to get more than this, inflation will increase – with wages accelerating and prices following them upwards. So stable inflation requires realistic behaviour at the bargaining table.

The cursed dole

Today's tolerance of unemployment would have astonished people in the 1960s. Despite having anything up to one worker in ten on the dole, many a government in Europe can now expect not merely to survive, but to win re-election boasting of its economic prowess. Everywhere voters and politicians have grown used to unemployment that is indefensibly high. Yet there is no great mystery about why unemployment happens, or how to reduce it. The only mystery is why an avoidable misery has proved so politically tolerable.

Since economics understands so little, the claim that unemployment is understood must seem outlandish. It is, none the less, justified. This week a new book by three British economists – Richard Layard and Richard Jackman of the London School of Economics, and Stephen Nickell of the University of Oxford – considers what their profession has learnt about the subject over the past 20 years. Few of their colleagues, please note, will disagree with the book's central findings. Economists at different ends of the political spectrum are often embarrassed to find themselves agreeing, by and large, on what causes unemployment and how to cure it. So do

not be fooled by manufactured controversy over details and footnotes. *Unemployment: Macroeconomic Performance and the Labour Market* convincingly refutes the idea that countries have no choice but to live with high unemployment.

The macroeconomics of unemployment looks discouraging. The evidence is clear that, for any economy, there is a rate of unemployment that is consistent in the long term with stable inflation. Economists call this the non-accelerating-inflation rate of unemployment, or NAIRU. At lower rates of unemployment, inflation accelerates; at higher rates, it slows down. The cliché that 'there is no long-term trade-off between inflation and unemployment' – a claim first made by Milton Friedman in the 1960s – is true. Governments cannot buy lasting jobs by tolerating higher inflation. If they try, their reward is higher inflation – and the unemployment they started with.

The trouble is that this stable-inflation rate of unemployment may well be much too high; it need not correspond to 'full employment', or anything like it. The challenge for governments, then, is to change the NAIRU. In the main, this is not a task for demand management, but for supply-side policies.

The NAIRU, in effect, is the rate of unemployment that is just sufficient to control pressure for higher wages. The thought is unpalatable, but unemployment does in this way perform a necessary economic service. It follows that, to lower the NAIRU, governments have to make unemployment more effective – so that a smaller amount of it will exert an equally powerful influence over wage-setting. This can be done in several ways. They boil down to one broad idea: the unemployed must become stronger competitors in the labour market.

Partly this means obliging them to compete. The new book says that 'the unconditional payment of benefits for an indefinite period is clearly a major cause of high European unemployment.' In Japan, where unemployment has consistently been much lower than in Western Europe, unemployment benefits stop after six months. America's unemployment has generally been lower than Europe's (though not as low as Japan's); its benefits stop after six months, too. Benefits in most European countries are of virtually unlimited duration. For many, this makes long-term unemployment a less frightening prospect than it should be. The longer people have been unemployed, the harder it is for them to compete in the labour market – so the NAIRU rises. Open-ended entitlement to unemployment benefit is bad policy.

Having obliged the unemployed to compete, it is crucial that governments equip them to do so. For years, Sweden's labour-market policy has been the most successful in Europe. Benefits stop altogether after 14 months, but during that time the unemployed are helped to find work. The means include well-staffed placement services (with an average caseload per official that is one-fifth of Britain's); high-quality training courses (enough to accommodate roughly 1% of the labour force); recruitment subsidies (including a wage subsidy of up to 50% for those unemployed for more than six months); and, if all this fails, a guarantee of temporary public employment.

It costs money. Sweden spends roughly seven times as much per unemployed worker on such measures as Britain – or roughly 1% of GDP. But it wastes much less on unemployment benefits. The net cost to taxpayers is small, at worst.

Policies that oblige and equip the unemployed to find jobs will work better if the labour market can be opened up to the new competition. That means scrapping all minimum-wage laws, since they stop the unemployed from getting into the market. It also means curbing union power, so that union members (and their wages) are not protected at the expense of those who would like to work for lower pay. The evidence shows that where unions are weak, unemployment is lower.

There is a complication, however. For any given amount of union power, unemployment is lower if unions and employers co-ordinate their wage bargaining either across industries or nationally. So weak unions, as in America, are fine. Strong unions that co-ordinate their claims, as in Scandinavia, seem to have worked well, too – though Germany's strong unions have destroyed thousands of jobs by forcing wages in eastern Germany towards parity with the west. What works worst of all is strong but uncoordinated unions, as in Britain in the 1970s.

This western experience contains many lessons for the reforming economies of Eastern Europe. Whatever happens, the next few years are bound to throw millions of East Europeans out of work. To keep those millions as low as possible, governments must avoid open-ended commitments to unemployment benefit. Instead, they should devote more of their limited resources to training and placement services (information about vacancies, help with relocation and so on).

For the West the lesson is this: the jobless rates of the 1960s have not moved permanently out of reach. Today's high unemployment may be chronic – but it is curable.

Source: *Economist,* 28 Sept. 1991

What ensures this? The answer is that there must be enough unemployment. Just enough unemployment will ensure that the **'target' real wage** demanded by the workers exactly equals the 'feasible' real wage. If there is 'not enough' unemployment, wages will be pushed too high and wage inflation will increase. Alternatively, if there is 'excess' unemployment, wage and price inflation will fall.

Let us trace out carefully what happens if the government creates so many jobs that unemployment falls below the NAIRU – to, say, 5 per cent. Wage bargainers push up wage inflation above expected price inflation. Firms provide this increase because they too underestimated the rise in wages, and so allowed their price mark-up over actual wages to fall. So rising inflation was the device that reconciled the behaviour of wage-bargainers and the marketing managers of firms. As James Meade has put it, *rising inflation is the only possible outcome if you try to get a quart out of a pint pot.* By the same token, it is only the rising inflation which made it possible for us to have more employment than at the NAIRU.

So we have now gone behind the crude assumptions of Figure 12, on page 26, to see *why* inflation rises when unemployment is 'too low': it is because low unemployment encourages unrealistic wage behaviour. Equally, if unemployment is very high, the unions get cowed, wages are too low a mark-up on prices, and inflation falls.

Some other concepts
Before analysing the historical experience we need to relate this framework to some of the other terms often used in the discussion of unemployment.

'Keynesian' unemployment
This means the excess of unemployment above the NAIRU – in other words, the unemployment caused by deficient demand rather than the supply-side factors.

All the remaining concepts refer to different forces bearing on the NAIRU.

Seasonal unemployment
Many industries, such as agriculture and construction, operate on a strong seasonal basis, with the result that in slack periods some workers become unemployed. Most of the statistics used by the government are seasonally adjusted, so that this kind of unemployment will not appear.

Frictional unemployment
Even if the economy were to be at 'full employment' there would still be

some unemployment. This apparent contradiction is explained by the presence of frictional unemployment. Workers leaving jobs often take a little time to find and start new ones, and new workers entering the labour market may stay unemployed for a time while they find out what jobs are available. This type of unemployment therefore represents the operation of the labour market in matching workers with jobs.

Structural unemployment

This aspect of unemployment results from changes in the industrial and occupational structure of the economy. The labour market may only respond slowly to these changes, which implies that in the meantime there are a number of workers who find their particular skills no longer in demand.

Classical unemployment

High unemployment may be associated with 'too high' a real wage. If this is so the unemployment is called 'classical'. Though there have been cases of this type, the more common reason why unemployment is high is that at a given unemployment level workers seek too high a real wage and unemployment has to rise to prevent them getting it.

KEY WORDS

Inflation	Overkill
Non-accelerating	Underkill
inflation rate of unemployment	Overheating
(NAIRU)	Supply side
Adaptive expectations	'Feasible' real wage
Commodity prices	'Target' real wage
Indexation	Money wage
Phillips curve	Price mark-up
Real aggregate demand	Monopoly

Reading list

Driffill, J., 'Inflation and the labour market', *Economic Review*, Jan. 1990.

Gavin, M., and Swann, P., 'Minimum wage debate', *Economic Review*, Feb. 1992.

Heathfield, D., Chapters 1, 3, 6 and 8 in *UK Inflation*, Heinemann Educational, 1992.

Malcomson, J., 'Unemployment: further understanding', *Economic Review*, March 1991.

Paisley, R., and Quillfeldt, J., Exercises 14, 23 and 24 in *Economics Investigated*, vol. 2, Collins Educational, 1992.

Essay topics

1 'Whether an expansion of aggregate demand increases employment or the price level depends upon the nature of aggregate supply.' Discuss. (Associated Examining Board, 1991)

2 'Unless someone has repealed the laws of supply and demand, I am afraid that the higher the price that is asked for labour, the less labour will be employed' (Norman Tebbit, when Secretary of State for Employment). Explain and critically assess this statement. (Associated Examining Board, 1989)

3 Explain what is meant by the 'natural rate' of unemployment. Evaluate the likely effects on the economic performance of the British economy of policies designed to reduce the natural rate. (Joint Matriculation Board, 1988)

4 Distinguish between voluntary and involuntary unemployment. Analyse effects of supply side policies on both of these types of unemployment. (University of London Examinations and Assessment Council, 1990)

Data Response Question 2
The UK labour market: equilibrium or disequilibrium?
This task is based on a question set by the Associated Examining Board in 1990. Read the article below, which is adapted from *Lloyds Bank Review* in July 1987, and answer the following questions.

1 How would equilibrium theorists explain the pattern of relative wage rates?
2 Why is frictional unemployment not regarded as 'evidence of problems in the labour market'?
3 Explain the differences between the equilibrium and disequilibrium theorists' views of the causes of unemployment.
4 Discuss the policies to reduce unemployment which are likely to be advocated by (i) equilibrium theorists, and (ii) disequilibrium theorists.

The labour market in this country is one of the most studied but probably least understood of all markets. There are a wide range of views about the nature of the labour market. On the one side there are the 'equilibrium theorists', who argue that the labour market is not dissimilar to competitive markets, like that for cabbages or foreign exchange. At least they say it has more in common with such markets than is commonly supposed. Thus the price in each market, be it cabbages or labour, is determined by the equality of supply and demand. Equilibrium theorists argue that real wages adjust quickly to changes in supply and demand.

An important part of the equilibrium approach is the explanation it suggests for the pattern of rising real wages and unemployment. The explanation advanced is couched in terms of upward (leftward) shifts in labour supply, these reductions in the supply of labour being the result of increases in the value of social security benefits and of increasing pressure on the labour markets by trade union activity. In an equilibrium model, measured unemployment is then explained by the rational supply decisions by workers, although it is also recognised that there will be frictional unemployment even in a competitive labour market. Such frictional unemployment is, of course, an almost inevitable feature of a flexible, changing economy, and as such is not evidence of problems in the labour market. In the main, the argument put forward by the equilibrium theorists is a supply-side explanation of changes in measured unemployment. Put another way, they argue that the natural or equilibrium rate of unemployment increased substantially during the 1980s, largely due to these supply-side effects.

The other or opposite view of the labour market is that it is more or less permanently in disequilibrium, with the supply of labour not being brought into equality with the demand, by smooth quickly adjusting real wages. According to this alternative, real wages are rigid, especially downwards. Hence a fall in the demand for labour, for example, will be reflected in an increase in unemployment, which is largely involuntary, and which will tend to persist. 'Disequilibrium theorists' generally advocate demand reflation as a means of reducing unemployment.

Chapter Three

The UK experience

'The government then sent for the fire brigade in the form of higher unemployment.'

So what is the explanation of our abnormally high level of unemployment? In the very short run, unemployment is determined entirely by the level of spending on British output – that is, it is determined by 'demand'. But over the longer run, as we have intimated in Chapter 2, it is necessary to take into account the 'supply side' of the economy: how much output can the economy supply without increasing inflation? It is this area that will be important in determining where the NAIRU lies. We shall argue that the rise since 1979 has been demand-led.

Up to 1979: supply-side forces
In the years up to 1979 there were a number of changes on the supply side which made it more difficult to maintain full employment without a wage explosion, so that the economy's NAIRU rose over the period. These factors included ● greater union pressure, ● wider access to the social security system, and ● higher taxes on jobs (National Insurance contributions). ● In addition there was the first oil shock of 1973–74 which made it more difficult to provide workers with the living standards they expected.

These factors tended to raise the 'target' wage relative to the 'feasible' wage, so that the NAIRU increased. For any rate of unemployment below this new higher NAIRU there is a tendency for the rate of inflation to increase. But this rise in inflation cannot continue indefinitely, and eventually the government allows unemployment to rise in order to dampen down wage pressure. Thus in the 1970s unemployment rose as a way of containing wage pressure. As we saw in Figure 13(c), inflation was reduced sharply by higher unemployment – and by incomes policy.

But by 1979 unemployment in the UK had risen only to 4 per cent – that is about $2\frac{1}{2}$ points above the full-employment level of the 1950s and early 60s. So that was the magnitude by which supply-side forces raised unemployment.

Since 1979: demand-side forces

After 1979 unemployment rose to over 10 per cent – a much bigger increase. This rise was 'demand'-led. It was caused by contractionary **monetary policy** and **fiscal policy,** and by the slowdown in world trade following on the second oil price rise. But Britain was by 1979 a major oil producer and hence uniquely well placed to escape the ill effects of the oil shock. Instead Britain led the collapse, with national output falling by 5 per cent between 1979 and 1981 – more than in any other country.

The motive for contractionary policies was the surge in inflation in 1979–80, which had occurred for three main reasons. ● First, the

RIDDELL

incoming government abandoned incomes policy and gave large pub-lic-sector pay rises. • Then there was the second oil shock. But, as an oil producer, Britain could have attempted to escape its inflationary effects by using the oil revenues to cut taxes. • Instead we did the reverse and increased VAT from 8 to 15 per cent. Inflation shot up, as the non-monetarists had predicted. *The government then sent for the fire brigade, in the form of higher unemployment.* Let us see what happened.

High exchange rates and tight money

As a result largely of tight money, the pound escalated to a level where it became impossible for whole sections of manufacturing industry to sell their goods at all. Between 1979 and 1983 employment in manu-facturing fell by 23 per cent. It has shown no sign of ever recovering. For most of the 1980s the level of the **Sterling Index** (a measure of the pound's value against a weighted basket of 17 other currencies) showed that the pound was being held at a level where British goods were much less competitive in world markets than in the average of the 1970s. Figure 15 shows this loss of competitiveness by looking at an

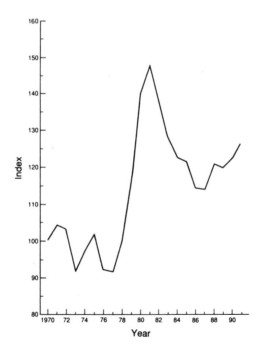

Figure 15 IMF Index of relative unit labour costs (1970–79 = 100)

index of relative unit labour costs (which compares the UK's labour costs per unit of output with that of a weighted average of its competitors' unit labour costs). The late 1970s and early 80s are associated with a massive increase in costs, which was only incompletely reversed over the mid-80s. In the last few years the index has risen substantially, further threatening export industries and making a recovery in manufacturing increasingly less likely.

Tight budgets

There was also a major squeeze on the budget. The share of taxes in national income was raised from 34 to 38 per cent, while government expenditure (as a percentage of potential output) remained virtually unchanged from 1979 to 1981. Similar squeezes happened in other major European countries, but the reverse happened in the USA. This provides a perfectly controlled experiment for the effect of budgetary policy. The results can be seen in Figure 16.

In Britain and the European Community the budget deficit (appropriately adjusted) was cut between 1979 and 1986 by 4–5 per cent of

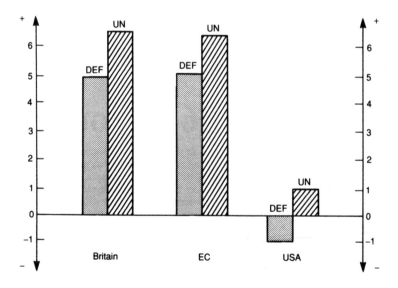

Figure 16 Unemployment and the public deficit (DEF = cut in adjusted budget deficit 1979–86, in percentage points; UN = increase in unemployment 1979–86)

national income, and unemployment by 1986 was over 5 per cent higher than in 1979. By contrast, in the USA the budget deficit was expanded, and there was no rise in unemployment compared with 1979. This shows clearly the power of budget cuts to destroy jobs.

The three hundred and sixty-four

In April 1981, the following letter was sent to *The Times* by 364 British university economists:

'We, who are all present or retired members of the economic staffs of British universities, are convinced that:
(a) there is no basis in economic theory or supporting evidence for the government's belief that by deflating demand they will bring inflation permanently under control and thereby induce an automatic recovery in output and employment;
(b) present policies will deepen the depression, erode the industrial base of our economy and threaten its social and political stability;
(c) there are alternative policies; and
(d) the time has come to reject monetarist policies and consider urgently which alternative offers the best hope of sustained economic recovery.'

This letter generated a large amount of interest. In November 1988, two of the economists wrote the accompanying article in *The Times*.

Were the 364 wrong?

We think it is unlikely that any of those who signed this statement fully appreciated the extent to which it would remain in the public consciousness. Even in 1988 ministers still make speeches referring to the 364 economists. Only a few days ago Sir Douglas Hague, the former chairman of the Economic and Social Research Council, commented that they ought to apologize to Mrs Thatcher.

Against this background, and at a time when the Government's economic policy appears to be confused, we thought that it might be interesting to assess the statement in the light of the government's economic record of the past seven years.

First, with reference to (a), we point out that a 365th economist would have supported our claim that monetary policy on its own could not produce a permanent reduction in inflation combined with a permanent reduction in unemployment. In 1968 Professor Milton Friedman, who provided the intellectual basis for Mrs Thatcher's policies, said that monetary policy could have no long-run effect on the level of employment and output. Indeed, no monetarist has ever been able to offer any convincing theory of why the long-run level of output and employment should depend on the rate of inflation. The output record of high-inflation countries such as France and Italy is not so different from that of low-inflation countries such as Germany and Switzerland.

What do we make of the government's record? There can be no doubt that inflation seems to be under control. But has there been an automatic recovery in output and employment? When we signed our statement there were 2,525,200 registered as unemployed. The number rose to more than 3.4 million in January 1986 and did not fall below the April 1981 total until May of this year. And the definition of unemployment has been changed frequently over the last few years. Any correction for this leads to the conclusion that there are still more unemployed than there were in April 1981. One reason suggested for this is that the long-term unemployed have become unemployable. We hope that the government's new training scheme will do something to rectify this.

The output record is more successful, although not as good as that during the Heath or Macmillan years. Some industrial sectors have been badly damaged. Car output is back to its 1959 level, and during the mid-1980s steel output fell to a level familiar from pre-war days.

We do not say that Mrs Thatcher's policies were solely to blame for this. Many would argue that the trade unions have plenty to answer for. But the facts do not provide evidence that the 364 were wrong. The only part of (b) on which we were incorrect was our prediction of social unrest. Economists should not step outside their area of professional competence.

There is a further issue to consider. We never claimed that recovery in output was impossible; only that the policies of 1981 would not lead to recovery. We observe that between 1981 and 1984 the money supply grew faster than the government planned in 1981. And the public sector borrowing requirement was larger. Any more detailed study would confirm the view that the government did take our advice in (c) and (d), and change its policies.

These changed policies undoubtedly contributed to the expansion which we have seen. But the main reason for the rapid growth in demand and output is that the British public has rejected at least one of the classic Victorian virtues: thrift. Under Mrs Thatcher, consumption has grown much faster than output. Time will no doubt tell whether this is a substainable pattern of expansion, but an interim judgement has to be that it is a good symptom of living beyond our means.

Very few of those who over the past seven years have attacked our statement have had an opportunity to re-read it. They probably have a blurred image of a bunch of left-wing Keynesians and proceeded to shoot from the hip. As it happens there is almost certainly a consensus of economists throughout the world that (a) is a correct statement. From a scholarly point of view we regret that somewhat dogmatic prediction in (b), not because it was wrong but because a careless reader like Sir Douglas Hague will misinterpret it. We were careful to say 'on present policies', and that caveat deserves attention.

We promise that should the balance of payments continue to deteriorate and inflation start up again we shall not claim to have been right. All we shall claim is that we made an honest assessment in 1981 based on such knowledge and understanding which serious economists have. One cannot ask for more.

Frank Hahn and Martin Weale

Inflation down but not falling

Thus tight money and budget cuts pushed up unemployment. At the same time they *did* cut inflation.) But inflation largely stopped falling in 1983. Since then underlying inflation remained stable for a long time at 4–5 per cent, and wage inflation at around $7\frac{1}{2}$ per cent. Towards the end of the 1980s both of these measures moved significantly upwards, although there has been a recent fall in both price and wage inflation. As of mid-1992, price inflation was 4 per cent and the annual increase in earnings was 6 per cent.

Why has wage inflation been high for so long?

There are three possible factors that could be important here. The first is the mass of long-term unemployed people (over 30 per cent of the unemployed) who have been out of work for over a year. They have largely given up hope of work, and are often considered as write-offs by employers. Thus an appalling situation has developed in which there is an unemployment culture of people who have given up hope. The Thatcher short sharp shock, which was meant to revitalize the country, has destroyed many peoples' working patterns and, through high unemployment, undermined the work ethic in large areas of the UK. In recent years the government has tried to reverse this situation through the **Restart Programme** of interviews, in which the long-term unemployed are offered advice and encouragement to further their job prospects.

The second factor is that the labour market is split into **insiders,** who are employed, and **outsiders,** who do not have a job but want one. Insiders bargain over wages, but they do so solely in their own interests, without considering the wishes of outsiders. In this case, when a shock leads to large numbers of workers becoming unemployed, they may stay unemployed because insiders will not lower wages in order to increase employment. Consequently wages will not fall when unemployment is high. This factor is probably not as important as the first.

The third factor is the mismatch between the skills demanded in the economy and the skills possessed by the unemployed. As Figure 17 shows, in the late 1980s skilled labour was as scarce as it was in the late 1970s (though less scarce than in earlier times). However, the slackening of the jobs market in the 90s has pushed the current figure for the shortage of skilled labour down to a near-record low. Furthermore, for workers without skills (like so many of the unemployed), the market remains as weak as ever. The government has tried to tackle this imbalance through **Employment Training** but, as we shall see, there is a long way still to go.

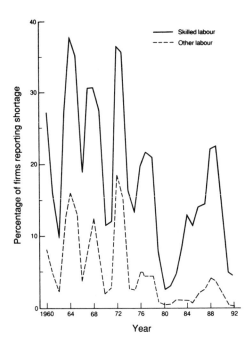

Figure 17 Shortages of skilled and other labour

The Lawson boom and the Lamont bust

During 1986–88 the British economy went through a strong period of expansion. The gross domestic product of the UK rose markedly in this period: by 4.4 per cent in 1987 and 4.3 per cent in 1988. This was caused by a surge in investment (starting from a rather low level) and a rise in consumer spending fuelled partly by easier borrowing.

As a consequence of this growth, **the workforce in employment** (the employed, plus self-employed, plus HM Forces plus those on work-related government training programmes) returned to, and exceeded, its 1979 level, as shown in Figure 18. Such a rise may not have implied an all-round rise in *employment* opportunities, however. Firstly this increase included a rise in the number on work-related government programmes from just 8000 in June 1983 to 376000 in September 1988. Secondly, although there was a great improvement in the number of jobs, much comment was made on the difference between the types of work that became available and the characteristics of the unemployed who were available to fill them (i.e. on the level of mis-match).

The jobs that were created in the late 80s were concentrated in the

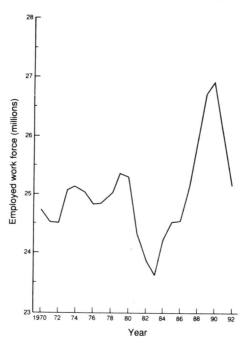

Figure 18 Workforce in employment in the UK

more prosperous southern regions, in the service industries, and included a large proportion of part-time positions. The rise in these jobs attractive to women can be argued to do little for the 'typical' unemployed worker of Chapter 1, who has a background in industry, is male and comes from the north of the UK. The change in the distribution of jobs over the 1980s is shown in the left-hand side of Figure 19. The greatest increases in employment from 1983 to 1991 came from females, with a rise of 1.5 million in employees in employment. Male part-time employment increased by only 330 000 over the eight-year period, but male full-time employment did even worse, falling by 660 000; so there has been a net drop in male jobs of 330 000 over the past eight years.

However, the growth of employees in employment is only half of the story. An important part of the change in the labour market in the 1980s was the growth of self-employment, from 1.8 million in 1979 to 3.1 million in 1991. The right-hand side of Figure 19 shows that the total number of self-employed grew by 900 000 between 1983 and 1991. It is conspicuous that the growth in self-employment over this period has been concentrated amongst males. Whether this is a

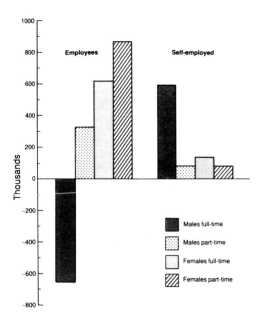

Figure 19 Employment change, June 1983 to 1991

response to the relatively poor performance of male jobs over the past decade is a moot point. The fast growth in employment in the late 80s led to a large fall in unemployment (see Figures 1 and 2) but to upward pressure on inflation (see Figure 13).

The party ended in 1990 and the economy has seemingly been suffering from a hangover ever since. Unemployment has risen from April 1990 until the time of writing, with only little indication of this growth stopping, let alone there being a return to the lower (although still high) levels seen in the late 1980s. The recent unemployment performance of the UK is considered at greater length in the following chapter.

It is striking, when looking at Figures 9 or 17 for example, how similar the early 1990s are to the early 1980s; and as Figure 20 shows, the unemployment experience of the 1980s was very like that of the 1930s. It is certainly to be hoped that macroeconomic policy can do better than to repeat persistently the unemployment performance of the 1930s Depression.

The basic point is this. High unemployment need not be a permanent evil, as the history of this and other countries over the twentieth century has taught us. As Figure 20 shows, unemployment in the

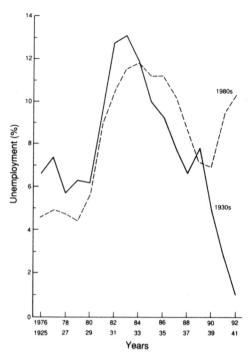

Figure 20 Unemployment in the 1930s and 1980s

1980s remained high for rather longer than it did in the 1930s, and now in the 1990s it is rising back towards very high levels again. Unless the government acts now, historians of the future will condemn their economic policies, as they now condemn the policies of the 1930s. The fact is that now, as then, many people can see no alternative to these policies.

KEY WORDS

Monetary policy
Fiscal policy
Sterling Index
Index of relative unit
  labour costs

Restart Programme
Insiders and outsiders
Employment Training
The workforce in
  employment

Reading list
Healey, N., and Levačić, R., Chapters 1, 5 and 6 in *Supply Side Economics*, 2nd edn, Heinemann Educational, 1992.

National Institute of Economic and Social Research (NIESR), Chapter 7 in *The UK Economy*, 2nd edn, Heinemann Educational, 1993.

Paisley, R., and Quillfeldt, J., Exercise 14 in *Economics Investigated*, vol. 2, Collins Educational, 1992.

Smith, D., Chapters 1, 6 and 7 in *Mrs Thatcher's Economics: Her Legacy*, 2nd edn, Heinemann Educational, 1992.

Essay topics
1 Discuss whether it is possible to have low unemployment at the same time as a low rate of inflation. (Associated Examining Board, 1990)

2 a) What do economists mean by the 'natural' rate of unemployment? b) How might 'demand-side' and 'supply-side' policies affect the 'natural' rate of unemployment? (Associated Examining Board, 1992).

3 a) What factors determine the level of aggregate supply in an economy? b) To what extent may reductions in unemployment benefit and income tax rates affect the general level of unemployment? (University of London Examinations and Assessment Council, 1993).

4 a) Distinguish between 'Keynesian' or 'demand-deficient' unemployment and other types of unemployment. b) Why might economies be prone to periodic demand-deficient unemployment? (Welsh Joint Education Committee, 1992)

Data Response Question 3

The UK economy 1985–91
This task is based on a question set by the University of Oxford Delegacy of Local Examinations in 1992. Study Table A (noting that the figures for 1991 were estimates at the time the table was published), and answer the following questions.

1 (i) Do the data in Table A provide evidence that the UK economy enjoyed a 'consumer boom' between the years 1985 and 1991? (ii) Drawing on the data provided, suggest possible reasons for the behaviour of consumer expenditure.

2 (i) Do the data suggest the existence of a relationship between unemployment and inflation? (ii) What economic explanation might there be for such a relationship?(iii) Do the data support the view

that a 'Phillips curve' type of relationship existed in the United Kingdom during this period?

3 (i) Describe and comment upon the nature of the relationship between UK's balance of payments current account performance and gross domestic product (GDP). (ii) Identify and briefly comment on any *three* factors, other than GDP, which might have played a part in creating successive current account deficits.

Table A The United Kingdom economy 1985–1991

	1985	1986	1987	1988	1989	1990	1991
Real GDP (1985 = 100)	100	103	108.1	113.1	115.7	117.1	115
Consumer expenditure (£bn 1985 prices)	217	229	241	258	268	273	271
Wages and salaries (£bn current)	165	179	194	215	237	263	286
Inflation % (RPI % increase on previous year)	6.0	3.5	4.1	4.9	7.7	9.5	5.8
Unemployment (millions)	3.0	3.1	2.8	2.3	1.8	1.6	2.2
Exports of goods and services (£bn current)	103	107	112	113	119	125	127
Imports of goods and services (£bn current)	99	106	114	128	140	142	138

Source: *Economics, Journal of the Economics Association,* spring 1990

Chapter Four

The rise in unemployment from 1990

'Being jobless is a price worth paying to beat inflation'. Chancellor of the Exchequer, Norman Lamont

The fall in unemployment ended in April 1990. This chapter applies the analysis developed in Chapter 2 to the subsequent rise in unemployment. First we set out the basic facts which we have to explain. In doing so we compare the early 1990s with the previous recession of the early 1980s. This enables us to assess the effects of the radical policies of the 1980s on the workings of the labour market.

The basic facts
The movements in employment and unemployment in the two years to March 1992 are set out in Table 5. This table uses the claimant count definition of unemployment (on the Labour Force Survey definition the labour force is the same in March 1990 and March 1992 and the rise in unemployment is greater).

The early 1990s initially appear very similar to the early 1980s. The largest contributions to the rise in unemployment have again come

Table 5 Changes in employment and unemployment

	March 1990 (millions)	March 1992 (millions)	Percentage change
Employees in employment			
Manufacturing	5.2	4.6	−10.4
Services	15.8	15.6	−1.1
Other sectors	1.8	1.6	−14.1
All employees	22.8	21.8	−4.2
Self-employed	3.3	3.0	−7.9
HM forces	0.3	0.3	−4.2
Unemployed and government training schemes	2.1	3.1	+47.2
Labour force	28.4	28.2	−0.9

Note: The other sectors are building, farming and energy.

from the decline of manufacturing and the loss of jobs in the building industry, which always suffers severely in recessions.

What has happened to unemployment

The rise in unemployment between 1990 and 1992 is, in fact, very different from that in the early 1980s, in particular because of its regional distribution. Figure 21 shows the regional increase in registered unemployment between May 1990 and May 1992. The total width of the bars represents unemployment in May 1992.

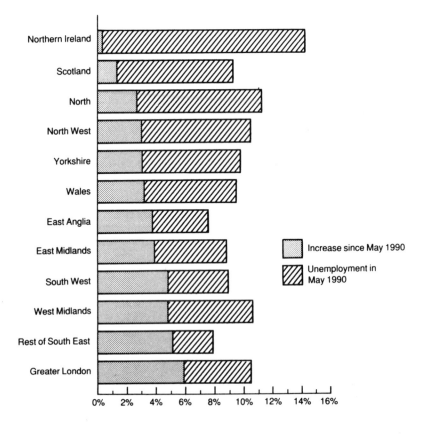

Figure 21 Unemployment in May 1990 and 1992 as a percentage of the labour force

The most striking point about the rise in unemployment in this recession is that it has occurred to a greater extent in areas with initially low rates of unemployment. The contrast between the regions of low and high unemployment is even more marked when one considers unemployment in May 1992 as a percentage of its level in May 1990. This figure ranges from 106 per cent in Northern Ireland to 285 per cent in the South East outside London, compared to 166 per cent in the entire UK. By way of contrast, in the recession of the early 1980s the rise in unemployment was generally higher in regions where unemployment was already high. *Thus the 1990s recession is much more egalitarian than that of the 1980s in the sense that regional differences in unemployment rates have faded rather than sharpened.*

Figure 9 shows that the movements in unemployment and vacancies in the early 1990s were very similar to those seen a decade earlier. Unemployment in the 1990s has risen rather less than in the early 1980s, while vacancies have fallen more sharply than ten years earlier. In fact the levels of both unemployment and vacancies in 1992, as well as the ratio of unemployment to vacancies, are very similar to those which prevailed in 1982. So, there are roughly as many unemployed now as there were a decade ago, and each unemployed person has about the same chance of finding a vacancy now as they did then. From 1982 unemployment rose for a further three years; it remains to be seen whether the current recession will follow a similar course.

What has happened to employment

Figure 22 shows the regional change in the number of employees in employment in the UK in the two years from March 1990. It is evident from this figure that the regional variation in the growth of employment and unemployment in the 90s has largely been driven by the changes in service employment. Employment in manufacturing and other sectors has declined in every region in the country, whereas service employment has been hit badly in the South East but has grown strongly in Scotland, the East Midlands and East Anglia. This contrasts sharply with the early 1980s, when the decline in manufacturing relative to other employment, which is shown in Figure 6, accounted for much of the change in employment in the UK, and indeed much of the regional variation in the growth of unemployment. For example, the West Midlands had the largest absolute rise in unemployment, reflecting the concentration of manufacturing in the region.

Self-employment

By the definition of the labour force, the rise in unemployment equals the

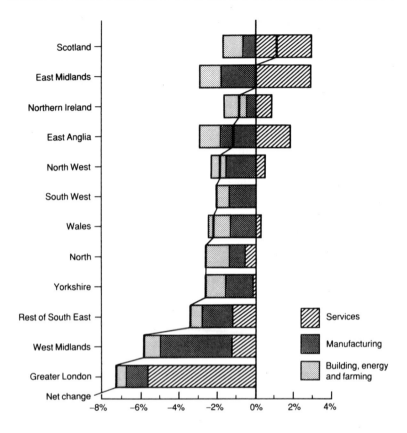

Figure 22 Employment change by region and sector in the two years to 1992, as a percentage of the workforce

change in the labour force minus the change in employees in employment minus the change in self-employment. Table 5 shows that the labour force fell by 200 000 between 1990 and 1992, whereas employees in employment fell by 1 million and unemployment rose by 1 million over the same period. Simple arithmetic (allowing for rounding error!) produces a figure of 300 000 for the fall in self-employment; this contrasts with the uninterrupted growth in self-employment from 1977 to 1990. The regional variation in self-employment is similar to that in the number of employees in services. In the two years to 1992 the change in self-employment ranges from a fall of 2 per cent of the total labour force in the South East outside London to a rise of 1 per cent in Scotland and Northern Ireland.

Reasons for the rise in unemployment
For the economics of the rise in unemployment we must look at demand and supply.

Demand side forces
When unemployment increases rapidly, it is natural to look first at the demand side for an explanation. Supply side factors, which determine the NAIRU, tend not to fluctuate sharply. The two obvious factors that have affected real aggregate demand are the exchange rate and interest rates.

The experience of the 1990s is somewhat different from that of the early 80s. Inflation rose steadily from 1986, and had accelerated markedly by 1989, which prompted the doubling in **base rate** from $7\frac{1}{2}$ to 15 per cent. Once again the government, frightened by the prospect of high and rising inflation, chose to put out the fire with a massive deflation. The Chancellor of the Exchequer, when accused by the Opposition of deliberately provoking a jump in unemployment, defended himself with the claim that 'being jobless is a price worth paying to beat inflation'. When he said this, in May 1991, unemployment had risen by over 500 000; currently the level of unemployment is over one million higher than at March 1990 and it is rising faster than even the worst months of the early 1980s.

The pound entered the European Community's **exchange rate mechanism** (ERM) in October 1990. The central banks of member countries are committed to maintain the exchange rate of each currency within fixed bands. One way in which central banks can affect exchange rates is by purchasing or selling currencies on the foreign exchange market. Of greater importance for our analysis of unemployment is the restriction membership imposes on interest rates in member countries. Interest rates must be such that there is sufficient demand for each currency from investors to keep the currencies within their ERM bands.

The exchange rate chosen for sterling within the ERM appeared to be such that interest rates had to be maintained at a high level in order to support the currency. *The British economy in the early 1990s thus faced the same combination of high exchange rates and high interest rates as in the early 1980s.* The effect of this combination was to curtail the demand for UK goods. A strong exchange rate ensured that goods from the UK were expensive in other countries (although it also delivered benefits in terms of lower prices of imported goods, helping to reduce the rate of inflation). At the same time high domestic interest rates dampened domestic demand by both firms and consumers. Consumer demand in the 1990s is especially responsive to the level of

'Being jobless is a price worth paying to beat inflation'

Chancellor Norman Lamont was at the centre of a political storm last night after he said the huge jump in unemployment was a 'price worth paying' to bring down inflation.

The Opposition branded his remarks a disgrace, and said the Chancellor couldn't care less for the unemployed.

Mr Lamont told the Commons: 'rising unemployment and the recession have been the price that we've had to pay to get inflation down.'

When Labour MPs jeered and yelled at him the Chancellor shouted over their protests, and continued his speech.

He insisted: 'that is a price well worth paying.'

The remarks came just hours after a rise of 84,000 in the jobless total was announced by the government. The unemployment total went up for the thirteenth month in a row, and is now almost 2.2 millio n. Nearly 570,000 people have lost their jobs over the last year, as the recession has started, especially in the South.

Source: *Today,* 17 May 1991

interest rates because individuals now find that it is more expensive to borrow money for consumption goods, and because so many individuals are tied to floating rate mortgages as a result of the boom in home ownership in the 1980s (see the box 'The changing face of the housing market').

By September 1992 it became clear that a weakening pound could not stay within its required band against the deutschmark. In a market where 90 per cent of transactions are pure speculation, a belief that sterling may have to be devalued was the cue for a mass sell-off of the currency. The UK government purchased sterling on the market and raised interest rates, but it was not enough to prevent the pound from dropping through its ERM floor and then being withdrawn from the ERM system. The logic of the market dictates that traders should sell a good when its price will fall; therefore a key factor in exchange rate stability is a belief in the value of a currency. Unfortunately reputation is also important in the foreign exchange market, and any further foray into the ERM may be repelled by speculators who now think that the pound is vulnerable.

At the time of writing the pound is floating at a level of DM2.50, which represents a devaluation of 15 per cent from its previous ERM parity. While some in the government will be anxiously watching for signs of inflation (due to dearer imports), the Chancellor of the Exchequer welcomed the chance to use the floating exchange rate as part of 'a British economic policy and a British monetary policy'. Certainly the boost that a cheaper pound gives to exports will be gladly welcomed at a time when unemployment is high and rising at a near record rate.

The changing face of the housing market

Just as much of the conversation at dinner parties in the late 1980s seemed to revolve around the joys of home ownership, the conversation since 1989 has been dominated by stories of huge mortgage repayments, bankruptcy and repossession. Some people say that there is nothing new in such a boom and bust cycle and that rollercoaster price behaviour has long been observed, at least since the extraordinary fads and panics of the eighteenth century. But is the housing market today the same as it was 20 or even 10 years ago? Recent evidence suggests not, and it seems that the changes in housing have important repercussions on government macroeconomic policy.

The first table below shows the changes in types of housing over the past 20 years. While the percentage of households that own their house outright has remained fairly stable, there has been a large rise in the percentage that own with a mortgage. The other side of the coin is the dramatic fall in the percentage that rent their house. Part of this shift from rental to ownership reflects the policy of council house sales to sitting tenants in the 1980s.

Housing trends

	House owned outright	House owned with a mortgage	House rented (public)	House rented (private)
1971	22	27	32	20
1981	23	31	36	10
1990	25	41	27	8

Source: General Household Surveys

This change in the housing market matters from our point of view because many mortgages are floating rate and thus the repayments depend on the rate of interest. This is not true for rent payments. Standard macroeconomic theory tells us that the interest rate matters because of the sensitivity of firms' investment to the price of borrowing. In addition, and of growing importance since the late 1970s, we consider the effect of interest rates in the housing market.

The second table below shows the effect of a one percentage point cut in the interest rate on mortgage repayments. The effect is to increase disposable income for all mortgage holders and thus to increase their consumption, which in turn increases GNP and employment. Of course, these savings must come from somewhere, and in this case it is the lenders (i.e. the people who save money in banks and building societies, plus these financial institutions themselves) who are losing out. However, evidence seems to suggest that these lenders have a lower marginal propensity to consume than do borrowers. Hence the effect of a cut in interest rates is to carry out a transfer from lenders to borrowers, with a resulting rise in consumption and a fall in savings.

How the cut affects mortgages – what you can expect to pay monthly

Loan size	Endowment (9.95%)	Saving	Repayment (9.95%)	Saving
£30 000	£186.56	£14.07	£212.17	£11.32
£50 000	£352.40	£26.56	£395.08	£21.99
£60 000	£435.31	£32.82	£486.53	£27.33
£100 000	£766.98	£57.81	£852.35	£48.67

Source: Leeds Permanent Building Society

Entry into the ERM did not involve a change in policy on interest rates and the exchange rate. This policy had been adopted in response to clear signs of **overheating** in the economy in the late 1980s. The two obvious signs of overheating were a rise in inflation and in the balance of trade deficit. *Overheating occurs when unemployment is less than the NAIRU (i.e. there is 'underkill').*

Supply side factors

The recent changes in the level of aggregate demand can explain the rise in unemployment in the 1990s. However the long-run level of unemployment must, as always, be explained on the supply side.

Unemployment at its lowest point was only just below 7 per cent on the Labour Force Survey measure. At this point demand was clearly above the economy's capacity to supply, as was shown by the rising rate of inflation and the increase in the balance of trade deficit. This suggests that the NAIRU is significantly more than 7 per cent. *The NAIRU in the early 1990s does not seem to be much different from the early 1980s.* At first sight this is extremely disappointing in view of the supply side policy measures which we outlined in Chapter 3.

The success and failure of employment policies

Supply side measures may still have been successful in preventing an increase in the NAIRU as a result of the very high unemployment of the 1980s. High unemployment generally means that the proportion of the long-term unemployed increases. As explained in Chapter 3, the long-term unemployed may give up hope of employment and stop looking for work effectively. Employers may be unwilling to employ them, particularly if they can easily recruit workers who are not suffering from long-term unemployment.

For these reasons the long-term unemployed are less effective than the short-term unemployed in searching for work and so play a smaller role in restraining wage inflation. *So, the NAIRU, at least in the short run (which may be several years), is higher the larger the proportion of unemployment which is long term.*

As indicated by Figure 4, the level of long-term unemployment was much higher at the start of the 1990s than at the beginning of the previous recession. If the NAIRU has not increased in the short term as a result, this may reflect the success of employment policies, such as Restart, introduced in the late 1980s. It seems that a fall in **search effectiveness** with length of unemployment is now less of a problem than in much of the 1980s.

So, there is some evidence of success of supply side policies directed at search effectiveness. Unfortunately, it is not clear that the same can be said of **training policies**. The quality of training available to the unemployed through Employment Training is less than with earlier schemes, although more now receive some form of training. The employment rate of those completing government training schemes is disappointing. *It seems that the training the unemployed receive is doing little to tackle the mismatch created by the change in the skills required of the labour force.* At a time of high and rising unemployment it is clear that microeconomic policies designed to increase the economy's capacity to supply without generating inflation have much to recommend them.

```
┌─────────────────────────────────────────────────────────┐
│                      KEY WORDS                           │
│                                                          │
│  Base rate                    Search effectiveness       │
│  Exchange rate mechanism      Training policies           │
│  Overheating                                             │
└─────────────────────────────────────────────────────────┘
```

Reading list

Healey, N., and Levačić, R., Chapter 2 in *Supply Side Economics*, 2nd edn, Heinemann Educational, 1992.

Heathfield, D., 'Monetary policy 1947–91', *Economic Review*, April 1992.

Helm, D., et al., 'Supply-side policy: success or failure?', *Economic Review*, April 1992.

National Institute of Economic and Social Research (NIESR), Chapter 7 in *The UK Economy*, 2nd edn, Heinemann Educational, 1993.

Smith, D., 'Why the 1990–92 recession has been different', *British Economy Survey*, Autumn 1992.

Essay topics

1 What evidence is there to suggest that Britain is currently experiencing a recession? (Oxford and Cambridge Schools Examination Board, 1991)

2 'Government policy of high interest rates has proved effective in bringing down the rate of inflation but only at great cost.' Discuss. (Oxford and Cambridge Schools Examination Board, 1990)

3 (a) What do you understand by the term recession? (b) Analyse the policies which a government could use to lift the economy out of recession. (University of London Examinations and Assessment Council, 1992)

4 (a) Outline the main macroeconomic objectives of the UK government in the 1990s. (b) Why do governments have difficulty in achieving these objectives? (University of London Examinations and Assessment Council, 1992)

Data Response Question 4

Conflict of economic objectives

This task is based on a question set by the Oxford and Cambridge Schools Examination Board in 1992. Study Figure A (from *Lloyds Bank Economic Bulletin*, July 1991) and Figure B (from *Fiscal Studies*, May 1991) and answer the following questions.

1 Outline and account for the significant features of the information in the two figures.
2 What conclusions can be drawn about the conflict of economic objectives since 1986?

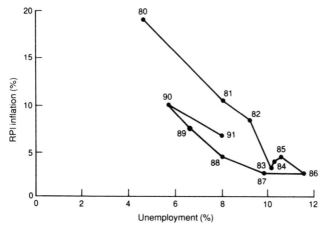

Figure A The inflation – unemployment 'trade-off'.

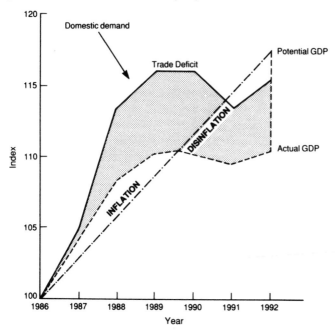

Figure B Index of potential GDP, actual GDP and domestic demand.

Chapter Five
Myths about unemployment

'... This argument is like the voice of the siren; it sounds sweet and reasonable, but it leads to disaster' Richard Layard

The previous chapter outlined our theory of why unemployment in the UK has been so high during the 1980s. Before we move on to consider various proposals for dealing with the problem, we shall analyse some rival explanations.

Myth 1: More technological unemployment

The first myth is widespread. Very many people believe that the rise in unemployment is due to modern technology, and for this reason they are deeply pessimistic about whether we could ever have full employment again. It is certainly true that machines are constantly replacing people, in task after task. But this cannot be why unemployment has increased so much recently. If changes of that kind caused higher unemployment then unemployment would have been rising since the beginning of time. Yet in fact there is no clear trend in unemployment, as Figure 1 showed.

There have been great **productivity** breakthroughs in the past but these have not led to prolonged general unemployment. We had the typewriter, the telephone, the electric motor, the internal combustion engine, the jet engine, and the plastics revolution. Particular workers often lost their jobs. But there was no general tendency to rising unemployment.

When **technical change** actually happens, there are of course changes in employment. Sometimes it goes up (as in the high-tech industries), sometimes it goes down (as with containerization in the docks). Either way there is some dislocation while new patterns of employment are established. But there is no evidence that high productivity growth has normally been a long-lasting source of difficulty. In the UK productivity growth was unusually high in the 1950s and 60s, as in much of the 1980s. But in the 1950s and 60s it caused no unemployment. It was when productivity growth fell in the 1970s that unemployment became a problem – owing to the difficulties of satisfying the demand for higher real wages and living standards. In fact the major country with the lowest unemployment is the one with the highest productivity growth – Japan.

But surely, you might say, high labour productivity (i.e. high output per worker) *must* be bad for employment in the economy. For if output does not rise and output per worker does, fewer workers are needed. But why assume that output does not rise? When it becomes possible to produce more output, the normal result is that more output is produced. This is what has happened over the centuries. The problem today is that output is low in relation to productivity.

The most basic fallacy in economics is the 'lump of output' fallacy: to take output as given. So let us ask instead why the actual output of the economy is lower than it could be. Some people say it is because of satiation – people now have all they need. That view is an insult to all those who live in shabby houses with ill-fed children. There may be some Hampstead trendies or busy stockbrokers for whom extra cash would do no good, but to talk of satisfaction in general is immoral. The fact is that output is low not because people do not want more, but because they do not have the money to spend. And the government worries about giving it to them, for fear of inflation.

Myth 2: Too many people

Many people think that unemployment is high because of the increase in the labour force (from immigration, for example). This is most unlikely. In the nineteenth century the labour force grew much faster than it has recently, with no increase in unemployment. Even in the period 1950–65 the labour force grew as fast as in the 1980s, and we now think of the former period as representing a 'golden age' for low unemployment.

In the short run various factors may influence the labour force and thus may lead to changes in unemployment. For example it could be argued that unemployment in the 1980s was exacerbated by two distinct factors. The first was the demographic influence of many more young people coming on the job market as one of the 'baby boom' generations started to turn sixteen. The other was the increased tendency of women to enter the labour force. Between 1981 and 1989 it is estimated that the activity rate of women in the UK – that is, the percentage of the female population who are either working or unemployed – rose from 47.6 to 53 per cent. This activity rate is projected to carry on rising, leading to a larger labour force. This rise, however, will be offset by a 'baby bust' as the number of school-leavers entering the labour market falls in the early 1990s.

The effects of the labour force on unemployment are short-term: the number of people is not a major factor in the long run. This is confirmed by looking at other countries. As Figure 11 showed, there has been a huge rise in the labour force in both the USA and Japan, but with no great change in unemployment. In the USA, both labour force and employment have risen by about 80 per cent in the last 30 years. The fact is that a normally functioning economy will find jobs for all the people around who want them.

Myth 3: Shortage of capital

So far we have disposed of two myths relating to the *long-term* trend of unemployment: it is not because of more technical change, nor because of too many people. We turn now to a more short-term issue. This is the common notion that unemployment has to be high today because there is not enough capital around to employ the whole labour force.

There can be occasions when this is a problem, as in post-war bomb-shattered Germany. Is it the case in the UK today? The best evidence comes from the answers which the Confederation of British Industry gets in its Survey of Industrial Trends. The CBI asks its members in manufacturing industry: 'Is your output over the next four months likely to be limited by shortage of capacity?' The answers are shown in Figure 23. These answers show that for the late 1970s and early 1980s

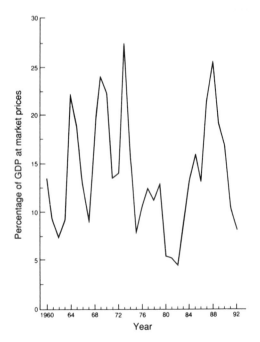

Figure 23 Firms limited by physical capacity

there was very little in the way of capacity constraints on firms; but with the rapid growth of the economy during the later 1980s these constraints became more important and reached a near-record level in 1988. However, in the years since the percentage of firms reporting a shortage of capital has dwindled towards historically low levels. In the early 1990s it seems that one would have to take a very gloomy view of capital shortages to view them as a major obstacle to putting the unemployed back to work.

Moreover, even if capital shortages were to be somewhat higher than they are currently there is no need for despair, because the notion of capacity is not in any sense absolute. Many different numbers of workers can be usefully employed with a given set of machines. In a given office block or restaurant, the number of workers present can be varied even more. On top of this, extra shifts can be worked. So the quantity of capital is never a continuing constraint limiting employment.

Myth 4: Unemployment would be lower if work was shared out more equally

This is another commonly held view. It states that if everyone were to work *shorter hours*, or *share jobs*, or *retire earlier*, then we could benefit from an immediate reduction in the numbers unemployed.

Let us consider the case for shorter **working hours** per week (the other cases can be analysed similarly). Suppose that the economy is going to produce a certain level of output, so that there are, roughly speaking, a certain total number of hours to be worked each week. If there are people unemployed then it would be better to reduce the hours worked by each worker and increase the number of workers. This would allocate work more fairly and it would reduce unemployment.

This argument seems plausible, but there is a critical assumption behind it which is often ignored. It is that output remains constant – or the 'lump of output' proposition. If we reconsider Figure 12, which showed the relationship between unemployment and inflation, then we see that whenever unemployment falls inflation rises more, or falls less, than it would otherwise. So using shorter working hours to cut unemployment leads to a rise in the rate of inflation over what would have occurred otherwise. Two responses are then possible.

Firstly, the government could accept the rising inflation. But if it were to do this then it would obviously have been better to cut unemployment by expanding output than redistributing the current amount of work.

Secondly, the government could decide that rising inflation is unacceptable and thus allow unemployment to rise to its former level. The shorter working hours will then have had no final effect on unemployment, but will have decreased output.

There then seems to be little theoretical use for arguing that shorter working hours (or **early retirement** or **job sharing**) present a valid case for reducing unemployment. And the evidence over the past fifteen years from a number of different countries shows that shorter working hours seem to be associated with greater rather than smaller rises in unemployment. A very similar picture can be drawn for the increase in early retirement and the increase in unemployment. Both theory and facts then seem to tell against this myth.

KEY WORDS

Technological
  unemployment
Productivity
Technical change
Labour force
Demography

Activity rate
Capital
Working hours
Early retirement
Job sharing

Reading list

Heathfield, D., Chapter 8 in *UK Inflation*, Heinemann Educational, 1992.

Layard, R., 'Pay leapfrogging', *Economic Review*, Sept. 1991.

Essay topics

1 (a) What is unemployment and how is it measured in the UK? (b) Analyse the main causes of unemployment in the UK at the present time. (University of Cambridge Local Examinations Syndicate, 1989)

2 Can increased government expenditure reduce unemployment in (i) the short run, or (ii) the long run? (University of Oxford Delegacy of Local Examinations, 1992)

Data Response Question 5

Productivity and pay

This task is based on a question set by the Joint Matriculation Board in 1991. Study the two articles from the *Times* and the *Financial Times*, and Table A, and answer the following questions.

1 Outline the arguments, as presented in the articles, for and against linking productivity and pay.
2 In the light of economic theory, how would you expect the relationship between productivity and pay to affect the level of employment and the degree of inflation in the economy? What support, if any, for your ideas do you find in Table A?
3 Is it possible to establish principles to ensure that payment to service sector employees is fair and efficient?

Table A UK manufacturing industry (1985 = 100)

	Employed labour force	Output per person employed	Average weekly earnings per head	Index of retail prices
1982	107.0	84.7	77.4	85.9
1983	102.1	91.8	84.4	89.8
1984	100.5	97.1	91.7	94.3
1985	100.0	100.0	100.0	100.0
1986	97.9	103.1	107.7	103.4
1987	97.0	109.9	116.3	107.7
1988	98.5	115.9	126.2	113.0
1989	98.5	121.6	137.2	121.8

Sources: CSO *Economic Trends*, July 1990; *Employment Gazette*, March 1990.

No return to a going rate

John Banham

The recent discussion of pay awards has a depressingly familiar ring. Ford is said to be setting a 'going rate' of over 10 per cent which will be followed by others, not only in manufacturing. 'Pay explosion,' scream the headlines. Ministers urge restraint and warn of the consequences of irresponsibility.

For the best part of 30 years successive governments sought to cajole employers towards a set figure for annual pay rises regardless of whether they had been earned or not. The result was a low-pay, low-productivity economy slipping inexorably down the league table of international competitiveness. The norm became an entitlement.

Only since the trading sector broke free of the going-rate mentality have we started to regain international competitiveness. Employers are constantly balancing the need to pay no more – and no less – than is required to attract and keep the necessary skills and commitment against the need to remain cost-competitive.

With the price of manufactured goods in the shops rising by around 4 per cent per year, it is clear that such a balance can be achieved only with improved performance. Since 1980, manufacturing productivity in Britain has risen by some 60 per cent overall, though with widely varying performances. The CBI's Pay Databank shows that employers expect to achieve further substantial improvement, on average of about 6 per cent, this year.

CBI data show that during the first half of the 1980s at least two-thirds of all firms linked pay to productivity, and the trend has continued since. Employment has risen to record levels, and, according to a recent consumer survey, there has been a perceived improvement in the quality of British-made goods. Export revenues (excluding oil) have been particularly buoyant; Britain's share of world manufactured exports is now rising, probably for the first time this century. It is not generally recognized that we export more, per head of population, than Japan.

All this shows what can be achieved when employers are free to build pay structures that suit their circumstances, and to pursue wage settlements that are financed by real improvements in performance. And at least one manufacturer in three is still achieving productivity improvements that outstrip the coresponding pay settlements.

To say this is not to under-estimate the difficulties of maintaining progress towards an internationally competitive manufacturing base, which holds the key to redressing our balance of payments deficit and curbing inflation. With poorer prospects for growth in the domestic market, manufacturers are having to redouble their export efforts to cover investment costs under a high interest rate regime. Since mid-1988, when interest rates took off, employers have also been grappling with inflationary pressures on pay.

Despite the improvement, the link between pay and performance is still not strong enough to ensure that in all cases unit labour costs fall year by year, as they must in a competitive world. If they do not, the result will be fewer jobs. That is why the CBI emphasizes that pay rises must always be linked to improved productivity. There can be only one going rate. It is for unit labour costs. And our international competitors have ensured that it must be negative.

Source: *The Times*, 18 Jan. 1990

The fallacy about productivity and pay

Richard Layard

Should workers be paid according to the productivity of their enterprise? According to senior ministers and CBI leaders the answer is Yes. But the standard answer has always been No.

So where do ministers go wrong? They start from the important proposition that to stop inflation, average wages in the economy should rise only as fast as average productivity. They then suppose that an easy way to achieve this would be if pay in each firm grew at the same rate as productivity in the same firm.

But this method is disastrous and doomed to failure. It is not only unfair but grossly inefficient. There are huge differences in productivity growth between sectors, which are mainly due to technological factors and not to the efforts of the workers. Thus some sectors have inherently greater productivity growth than others – with manufacturing generally outstripping services. Since this reflects no special merit among the workers in manufacturing, why should workers in services increasingly fall behind?

The service workers will not, of course, agree to do so, and market forces are on their side. So the chief result will be additional inflationary pressure, as service workers' pay tries to keep pace with manufacturing. This is the fundamental problem behind the ambulance workers' dispute.

The mechanism can be simply illustrated. Suppose productivity grows at 5 per cent a year in 'manufacturing' and 1 per cent in 'services' – an average of, say, 3 per cent. If all workers get 3 per cent wage increases, all will be well. But that is not the current philosophy. Government ministers have told those in 'manufacturing' that they can reasonably expect more. But then the 'service' workers also insist on getting more too. The result is disastrous.

An important reason for our present problems is this half-baked philosophy. Yet these issues are not new. In 1967 William Baumol wrote a famous article in which he explained how economic progress proceeds in a properly functioning economy. Productivity grows faster in manufacturing than in services. But wages grow at the same rate (so that the relative price of manufactures falls).

In this way the fruits of high productivity growth are spread evenly across the economy, not hogged by one group of workers. Thus barbers are four times richer than they were half a century ago because of productivity increases in the rest of the economy. How on earth could anybody believe that efficiency or equity required otherwise?

The inefficiency in productivity-based pay is manifest. If firms with high productivity growth pay higher wages, rather than cutting their prices, their sales will be depressed. Employment in the most productive sectors will be held back, and the least productive sectors (paying lower wages) will continue to waste labour. In international competition the country will be increasingly forced to specialise in low-productivity, low-wage industries.

This is the opposite of what would happen in a proper competitive labour market. Under competition, workers of a given type would be paid the same regardless of who employed them. And this would ensure that as a nation we best exploited our international comparative advantage.

Source: *Financial Times*, 31 Jan. 1990

Chapter Six
Remedies for unemployment

'Few people at Westminster retain much faith in remedies at a macro-economic level.' The Economist, June 1992

What can be done about unemployment? As we argued in Chapter 2, unemployment is determined by supply factors in the medium term and by demand factors in the short term. To reduce high unemployment there must be an increased demand for labour.

But it is no good if this demand simply spills over into higher wages and prices, rather than into jobs. Thus there must be **targeting** of the extra demand towards the slack part of the economy. Viewed in this way the policy also improves the supply capacity of the economy. Two other measures are also important steps in a programme of improving supply performance. The first is an attack on the lack of **training** in the British labour force; and the second is a willingness to tackle inflationary pressures directly through an **incomes policy**. Finally, we need to be sure that in the short run we can avoid an inflationary trade-off due to a speculative attack on the currency. This calls for a suitable **monetary policy**. Let us take these points in turn, beginning with a fuller statement of the problem, and then the four remedies.

The problem

It is not enough for the government to create jobs by spending money itself or by letting private citizens spend more (following tax cuts). It also needs to make sure that the spending does not lead to more inflation. Operating on demand without doing anything about the supply side will soon lead to bottlenecks which will affect inflation. For when unemployment falls, employers will find it more difficult to fill their vacancies. So they will try to attract workers by paying more than the going rate. At the same time unions will feel in a stronger position to push for wage increases, so wage inflation could be a very real problem, leading eventually to higher prices in the shops.

There is also another potential source of inflation. If we try to expand the economy, fears of subsequent inflation could undermine confidence in our currency. This could led to a fall in the value of the pound, so that we would have to pay more in pounds for anything that we imported. Thus prices in general would tend to rise and the original fears be confirmed.

Our policy should then be to increase demand by only as much as is justified by improvement in the supply side, otherwise lower unemployment will be associated with rising inflation. A strategy for cutting unemployment could achieve this if it takes heed of four basic principles.

Principle 1: Create jobs for the kind of people who are unemployed

It is dangerous to increase spending across the board, so that firms are trying to hire, say, more accountants as well as operatives: accountants are scarce while operatives are not. If vacancies are created for the groups who are already fully employed, then firms will bid up wages, leading to higher inflation.

To avoid this, extra spending must (as far as possible) be targeted towards people who would otherwise be unemployed. This means people who are actually unemployed, or those who are in high-unemployment groups – the young, those in high-unemployment areas, or semi- and unskilled workers.

For long-term unemployed people – a right to work and train

The group most needing help amongst the unemployed are the 33 per cent who have been out of work for over a year. The evidence suggests that such long-term unemployment does nothing to restrain inflation, because most **long-term unemployed** people are so discouraged and stigmatized that they are no longer part of the effective supply of labour as perceived by employers. Most of these people are not near retirement – only 20 per cent are over 50. The majority are in the prime of life, people who would be the backbone of a properly functioning economy. The top priority is therefore to bring the long-term unemployed back to work. To do so would be good economics in terms of both equity and, via the investment in the productive capacity of the country, efficiency.

This requires that such people be given preferential treatment in the allocation of jobs. For example, all employers could be offered a financial inducement for taking long-term unemployed people into regular employment – say £50 per week for the first twelve months of their employment (making £2500 altogether). Such a **job subsidy** would provide employers with an incentive to hire the long-term unemployed instead of other candidates. It is entirely possible that the social benefits to the economy (in terms of equity and efficiency) from the hiring of a long-term unemployed person will outweigh the necessary subsidy.

But justice and efficiency both suggest that we should go further and

establish for long-term unemployed people a **right to work or train.**
This is the situation in Sweden. There, after 300 days of unemployment, every unemployed person has a right to be offered work or
training. The training is high-quality: it costs (per place) $2\frac{1}{2}$ times
what is spent on Employment Training in this country, so that ex-
trainees are well prepared for modern industry, and are snapped up by
employers. The jobs are either subsidized jobs in the private sector or
public sector jobs on construction projects or in caring activities. By
this means unemployment in Sweden has never stayed above 3 per
cent and the unemployment culture has never developed. Such a
scheme costs money, and in 1986 the Swedish exchequer spent 2 per
cent of national income on training, employing and placing unemployed adults – compared with $\frac{1}{2}$ per cent in Britain. But in Britain we
spent 2.5 per cent of national income on unemployment benefits compared with 1 per cent in Sweden. So the Swedish 'employment principle', as they call it, has justified itself even in terms of purely public
accounting, let alone in terms of the social benefits that low unemployment brings. The cost of a right-to-work policy is not too vast and its
benefits in terms of human well-being and increased production would
be significant. This job guarantee could not only cut the current level
of unemployment, it would also ameliorate the effects of future recessions. The scheme presents a viable claim on government resources.

If Britain had a similar scheme, it would be essential that the jobs
available be proper jobs, paid at the going rate. The long-term unemployed want full-time jobs and there is certainly plenty of work that
needs doing. There is a massive backlog of housing maintenance and
repairs. We also have under-maintained hospitals and schools, and an
often sordid environment. And we have lonely and disturbed people,
needing home help and community care. In terms of economics, it must
promote efficiency if we bring together those needing work with the
work that so desperately needs to be done.

For the high-unemployment regions – a cut in National Insurance contributions

We can also consider special measures to stimulate employment in the
high-unemployment regions. Of course money spent on assuring the
right to work will automatically find its way to where the unemployed
people are. But there is a case for a more general measure. Subsidizing
capital is not the right way to proceed if we wish to secure more
employment – we need to reduce the cost of labour. One way to cut this
cost on a regional basis would be to reduce the employers' **National
Insurance contributions** in high-unemployment areas.

For low-paid people – a cut in National Insurance contributions

More than half the unemployed are semi- or unskilled, and this is one reason why they are unemployed. For as a result of modern technology, the relative demand for low-skilled people has fallen sharply (this could be thought of as a case of structural unemployment). Thus, if employers pay a living wage, they will simply not want to employ all the available labour.

There are two possible solutions to this excess of supply over demand. One is to force wages down and supplement pay substantially via Family Credit (and an equivalent for people without children) so that the low-skilled do not suffer. The other is to pay a reasonable gross wage, but ensure that other labour costs for these workers (from employees' NICs) are negligible. Given the economic and political difficulties of bringing down wages for a particular group of workers, the second route is probably preferable. But even that may not solve the whole problem. In this case a wide-ranging scheme of benefits is needed to ensure that, if wages do fall, the living standards of poor people do not.

Under the present tax and benefit regime there is an **unemployment trap** for many of the unemployed, whereby taking a low paid job is not significantly better than remaining unemployed. Table 6 presents an example where a low paid job only pays £8 per week more than the total of benefits received while out of work.

For reasons of equity one thing cannot be contemplated. We cannot consider denying benefits to people who refuse work which gives them

Table 6 The unemployment trap

Out of work		In work (stacking shelves in supermarket)	
Former earnings	£120.00	Gross earnings	£120.00
Unemployment benefit	£66.95	Tax	(£5.89)
Family credit	£26.41	National insurance	(£7.16)
Child benefit	£16.75	Family Credit	£26.41
Rent rebate	£18.26	Child benefit	£16.75
Comm charge benefit	£5.73	Rent rebate	£0.00
		Comm charge benefit	£0.00
		Travel to work	(£8.00)
Net income	*£134.10*	*Net income*	*£142.11*

Based on married couple with children aged 4 and 6

lower net income than they get on benefits, even if the economy would be more productive as a result. To help people out of the unemployment trap, either work needs to be made more attractive or unemployment less attractive. It is difficult on fairness grounds to justify cutting unemployment benefit, especially as this punishes all of the unemployed who are not in the unemployment trap. Instead we should expand employment that provides a reasonable living standard. This means, first, reducing any extra labour costs to an employer when he employs low-skilled labour; and second, supplementing the income of the workers if the wage is low.

Principle 2: Train everyone
If unemployment arises because of insufficient demand for low-skilled people, one approach is to help direct demand at those with limited skills, as we discussed in Principle 1. The other is to make the low-skilled people high-skilled. This means training not only the unemployed, which we have already discussed, but also (even more importantly) the employed, so that their skills remain up to date and in demand.

There is certainly a great deal of opportunity for training. By international standards we are a grossly under-trained nation. For example, in Britain 30 per cent of the labour force have absolutely no qualifications, compared with under 1 per cent in Germany. Whose fault is this? In Germany the training is mostly provided and financed by firms. But experience shows that British firms will not do the job on the proper scale, and half the firms rely on the others to do the training and then poach the trained labour. How can we change the system so that there is an incentive to provide training?

One obvious approach is (within each industry) to tax heavily the firms which train less than the industry average, and use the proceeds to subsidize those who train more than the average. This will provide an incentive for all firms to train more. As it stands the scheme is self-financing and need cost the government nothing, although a certain amount of policing may be necessary. In addition we could, as in Germany, require every employer to provide every employee under 18 with at least 8 hours off-the-job training a week.

This brings us briefly to **education,** which lays the foundation for a trained workforce. The UK's record here is not good either – we have fewer people aged 16–18 in full-time education than almost any other country in Europe. We shall only mention two possible measures to encourage more widespread education. The first is to increase the attractiveness of staying on at school via more sixth-form places, better quality teaching, a wider range of subjects, and so on. The second is to operate a financial inducement by providing a grant to 16-year-olds who stay at school for further education.

So there are plenty of things that could be done, given the money. But there remains the fear that, if we really did expand the economy, even with the maximum of targeting, inflation would still edge up. And the closer the economy came to full employment the worse the inflationary pressure would become.

Principle 3: Incomes policy

Incomes policies are national deals limiting the growth of wages. We have of course had incomes policies before. They have on occasion done good service. In particular, between October 1975 and October 1977 annual wage inflation was brought down from a terrifying 29 per cent to only 8 per cent. This was achieved by incomes policy with no increase in unemployment. By way of contrast, Mrs Thatcher's great reduction in inflation was rather less than that, and achieved at the cost of nearly two million extra people unemployed.

However, the incomes policy of the late 1970s was by no means perfect. It was too rigid to last, for it set an absolute limit to the pay increases for every group. This in effect suspended free collective bargaining, the negotiating process by which employers and unions reach agreement. It was therefore unacceptable to unions, who see collective bargaining as their raison d'etre. It was also unacceptable to firms who like to use flexible pay as a method of recruiting, retaining and motivating their workforce. In 1978 and 1979 the policy therefore began to falter.

Any future incomes policy would have to be more flexible in order to avoid these pitfalls. The obvious approach is one based on financial incentives. For example, we can imagine a policy with no absolute limit to pay increases, but which specifies a norm, which applies to the average pay in a firm. The firm can break the norm by awarding large pay rises, but only at a substantial cost to itself. Suppose, for example, the norm were 3 per cent. A firm that raises its average pay by only 3 per cent incurs no penalty. But a firm that raises its pay by 5 per cent would pay a tax equal to, say, the whole of its overpayment. It would thus pay to the Chancellor a tax equal to 2 per cent of its wage bill. This would make firms much more cautious in giving wage increases.

Even if the norm was breached by, say, 2 per cent on average, price inflation would remain constant, given 2 per cent productivity growth and a norm equal to the rate of price inflation. A scheme like this could be easily administered through the Inland Revenue, with a firm assessing its own liability and returning its cheque each time it paid its PAYE.

Before any policy were introduced we imagine that there would be intensive discussion with the TUC and the CBI in order to incorporate the interests of both sides. One would hope then that the norm could be a matter of agreement between workers and firms.

There may well be other better alternatives, but there is no way of ignoring the potential inflationary consequences if we intend to substantially reduce unemployment.

The aim is *not* to reduce real wages. It is simply to avoid the pointless increase of *money* wages and prices by the same amount. It would be an awful verdict on any society if it had to maintain a large proportion of its workforce unemployed, just because it could think of no better way of avoiding the wage–price spiral.

Principle 4: Defend the pound, where necessary, by interest rates

The above three principles have described one way, via targeting and an incomes policy, in which unemployment may be reduced without an eruption of domestic wage inflation. The bases are not all covered yet, however. There is always the danger that the **foreign exchange** market will have a sudden panic, forcing down the value of the pound. This would mean that the pound buys fewer deutschmarks. So more pounds would be needed to buy German goods. The result would be higher prices in the shops.

One way to avoid such changes in the value of sterling is to lock it into a fixed exchange rate system, such as the ERM. However, the pound's experience within the ERM was not a happy one (see Chapter 4) and at least in the near future it seems likely that the pound will float on the foreign exchange market.

The government has two ways to defend the pound. It can buy pounds in exchange for foreign currency. This reduces our foreign exchange reserves, and its effects cannot always be relied on. A more reliable approach is to raise interest rates. This makes foreigners more willing to lend money to Britain. For this purpose they have to buy pounds. So the flight from the pound is reversed, and its value recovers. (In fact, in the summer of 1992 there was a widespread belief that the level of domestic interest rates was being determined to a large extent by the need to keep the pound within its band in the ERM.) Experience has shown over and over again that this method works. Provided we are willing to use it (and known to be willing), there is no reason why the value of the pound should cause us problems. To put the matter another way, since higher interest rates go with less money, we must be willing to contain the growth of our money supply when this is needed to protect the exchange rate.

When President Mitterand tried to reduce unemployment by expanding the French economy in 1982, he did not follow this rule, and he also scared the financial markets with big wage increases and a programme of nationalization. There is no reason to believe that with an appropriate monetary policy, the outcome could not have been more successful.

This does not mean that the present exchange rate is sacrosanct. We are now running a balance of payments deficit on the current account. If we deliberately expanded our economy, the gap between imports and exports would widen further. Does this matter? Should we allow a weaker pound, in order to balance the current account? We should be wary of any uncontrolled depreciation of sterling, because too sharp a fall would add further inflationary pressure to the economy. But the Sterling Index for most of the 1980s and the 90s to date has stood at a level much higher than that of the 1970s. Some weakening of sterling would then help to restore competitiveness to UK industry.

KEY WORDS

Targeting	Right to work or train
Training	National Insurance
Incomes policy	contributions
Monetary policy	Unemployment trap
Long-term unemployment	Education
Job subsidy	Foreign exchange

Reading list

Bazen, S., and Thirlwall, A. P., Chapter 6 in *Deindustrialization,* 2nd edn, Heinemann Educational, 1992.

Donaldson, R., and Farquhar, J., Chapter 13 in *Understanding the British Economy,* Penguin, 1988.

Healey, N., and Levačić, R., *Supply Side Economics,* 2nd edn, Heinemann Educational, 1992.

Malcomson, J., 'Unemployment: explanations and remedies', *Economic Review,* Jan. 1991.

Paisley, R., and Quillfeldt, J., Exercise 31 in *Economics Investigated,* vol. 2, Collins Educational, 1992.

Whynes, D., Chapter 3 in *Welfare State Economics,* Heinemann Educational, 1992.

Essay topics

1 'The United Kingdom's taxation and welfare benefits systems have trapped the low-waged in relative poverty and the un-waged in unemployment.' Explain the causes of this situation. Explain how problems created by this situation might be reduced. (Associated Examining Board, 1991)

2 What is the purpose of an incomes policy? For what reasons might the UK government be reluctant to use such a policy? (Joint Matriculation Board, A/S level, 1992)

3 What are the causes of unemployment in the UK? Explain and evaluate the measures you would advocate to reduce the level of unemployment in the UK. (University of Cambridge Local Examinations Syndicate, 1991)

4 Why do skilled workers normally earn more than unskilled ones? Argue the cases for the training of skilled workers being financed by (i) the worker, (ii) the firm, and (iii) the government. (University of Oxford Delegacy of Local Examinations, 1991)

Data Response Question 6

The Charter for Jobs

This task is based on a question set by the Welsh Joint Education Committee in 1987. Reproduced here is an abstract of a report of a debate at King's College London (published in *The Times* on 6 November 1985). Read the abstract carefully and then answer the questions.

1 Explain the differences in the views of Layard and Batchelor regarding the underlying causes of the high unemployment prevailing in 1985.

2 Explain why Layard argues for a budgetary relaxation and why Batchelor considers that such a policy would not affect unemployment permanently.

3 Batchelor argues for 'microeconomic policies' to tackle unemployment (final paragraph). What do you think he means by this?

4 For what reasons did Layard mention the possibility of high interest rates as an argument against the effectiveness of budgetary expansion (final paragraph)? Why did he discount this argument?

5 Why did Layard consider that a fall in the exchange rate could lead to an 'upward twist in the inflationary spiral' but that a sufficiently tight monetary policy could sustain the exchange rate?

Richard Layard puts the case for Charter for Jobs

Our purpose is to show that there is a genuine alternative to present policies. Since 1979 unemployment in Britain has grown by 8% of the labour force – twice as much as the average for France, Germany and Italy. The basic reason is that the government's present budgetary stance is deflationary. We are desperately in need of budgetary relaxation.

But won't this simply unleash inflation? There are really three possible arguments against our policy. The first says there will be a wage explosion; the second says there will be a collapse of the exchange rate; the third says interest rates will sky-rocket.

The inflation issue is a serious one. Charter for Jobs is quite explicit about additional policy instruments. It says that 'if it proves impossible to reduce unemployment below present levels without inflation increasing, we would all consider some comprehensive approach including income and price policy to be better than doing nothing to reduce unemployment'. As for the argument about the exchange rate, it is true that an uncontrolled fall in the rate would lead to an upward twist in the inflationary spiral. But we know that the exchange rate can always be sustained by a sufficiently tight monetary policy.

The prediction that interest rates will soar depends of course on the underlying (government) debt situation. If all we did was to maintain the debt/income ratio we could afford a borrowing requirement of at least £11 billion compared with the £7 billion currently planned.

Ray Batchelor argues against higher spending

The policies advocated by the Charter for Jobs represent the latest embodiment of what I call 'nice-guy' economics. The hearts of the proponents are in the right place – they see a trade-off between unemployment and low inflation; they observe a mix of high unemployment and low inflation emerging from present policies and they want to reverse these priorities and buy lower unemployment at some cost – though as little as possible – in terms of rising inflation.

I share the concern of the Charter economists about the rate of unemployment. But I regard the causes as microeconomic rather than macroeconomic, the culmination of long-term trends rather than the short-term consequences of a monetarist experiment. The history of the past three reflations is hardly encouraging. Reflation in general succeeded in reducing or at least stabilising unemployment for a year or two but was followed by an inexorable rise of unemployment to yet higher levels.

Inflation cannot, even under ideal circumstances, make a permanent impression on unemployment. Over the long term the two are unconnected.

The history of the past three incomes policies has been no less discouraging than the record of the last three reflations. All have broken down. And all have been followed by an inflationary explosion as the price level re-established its underlying trend.

Butter mountains and wine lakes, most economists agree, arise because the price of these products has been maintained at high levels. Where we observe an army of unemployed workers our first thought should similarly be that the price which they are demanding for these skills is too high. My view is that a progressive mispricing of labour has arisen because of trends in both demand and supply sides. Since unemployment has these microeconomic rather than macroeconomic origins it must be tackled through microeconomic policies.

Chapter Seven

The objections considered

'No government can guarantee full employment' Lady (then Mrs) Thatcher

---

We have outlined some ways in which unemployment may be reduced without rekindling inflation. Even so a major programme for training, education and employment would inevitably involve some net cost to the state. Some people would say that we cannot afford it.

Objection 1: Spending on employment and training is self-defeating: it causes inflation and/or raises real interest rates

This is a widespread view and needs to be tackled head-on. Would there be detrimental effects on **wage inflation,** or on the **balance of payments,** or on the public finances, and thus on **real interest rates?**

We can start with wage inflation. The aim of the policies discussed in Chapter 6 is to increase the supply potential of the economy. If the policies increase the effective supply of labour (as they aim to), then an equal increase in the demand for labour can take place without an adverse effect on wages.

The balance-of-payments effects are less straightforward and depend on how the spending programme is financed. If the programme were financed by the government's foregoing planned cuts in income tax, it would actually help the balance of payments; for programmes of training, education, community care and construction all generate far fewer imports than the (first-round) spending induced by tax cuts costing the same amount. And, for the same reason, the number of jobs guaranteed in Britain is much higher. Thus if the programme replaced some policy of equal cost but higher import content, it would actually help the balance of payments. There may be further beneficial effects on the balance of payments if the exchange rate is used as a policy tool. A lower real value of sterling will encourage employment within the traded goods sector by making British exports more attractive. Further, as we argued in Chapter 6, a weaker pound will allow lower real interest rates.

What about a programme of job creation funded by public finance? If, as mentioned above, this employment programme replaces a current spending programme of equal cost, then there need be no effect on government borrowing (the **public sector borrowing requirement** or PSBR).

Even if this were not to be the case, so that government borrowing rose somewhat because of job creation, it is not clear that there would be any large effect on interest rates. If we look at the creditworthiness of the British government as it borrows money, it is clear that there are at least three important factors. The first two of these are the amount borrowed (i.e. the PSBR) and the ability of the government to repay the loan (in the same way, a bank considering a customer for a loan would want to know both the amount of the loan and the customer's income). In terms of ability to repay, the British government is currently in a strong position. For our 'national debt' (i.e. **government debt**) is now lower (relative to national income) than in most of the last two centuries. It has fallen sharply since the Second World War, as Figure 24 shows. In this case a moderate budgetary expansion would not raise this ratio alarmingly, and thus as a result of an employment programme financial markets would not insist on any major rise in long-term real interest rates, which are in any case largely determined at a common world level.

The third relevant factor when considering the financial market's response, via interest rates, to the government's debt position concerns

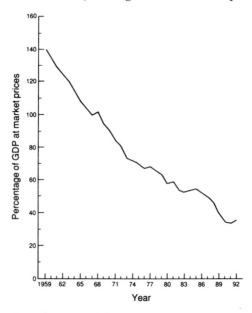

Figure 24 Public sector debt

the potential use of the money borrowed: there should be no reason why the government may not borrow money for projects which automatically pay for themselves in money coming back to the Exchequer. This applies to most of what is normally called public investment, as well as to much of education, health and road-building, which increase the country's tax base. Debt corresponding to genuine government investments could in principle be excluded from our calculations of the net debt to arrive at a figure for non-productive debt (say). We could then imagine that it is this non-productive debt which affects interest rates in the market. There is then a case for arguing that, as a productive investment, spending to reduce dole cheques will have less effect on interest rates than if the money were to be spent on other, less productive, causes.

Using this kind of argument it is less likely that a programme of this kind would crowd out other valuable investment projects in the economy. We have also argued that the effect on inflation is designed to be small, and that the balance-of-payments effects could be beneficial.

Objection 2: The unemployment problem is no longer serious

This is an insidious argument. It amounts to saying that if a patient's temperature falls from 105° to 104° he is no longer ill. This is what happens if the unemployment problem is judged not by how severe it is but by how it is changing. Of course, if we could guarantee that the changes will continue rapidly in a certain direction for some time to come, then the argument has some validity. However, it is obvious from Figure 1 that there is little trend in unemployment, so that the future movements of the unemployment rate cannot be relied on. Thus we can argue that the **unemployment level** is more important than the current *rate of change* of unemployment.

Unemployment – no end in sight

The official total for unemployment now stands at 2.72m. A leaked Whitehall document earlier this year suggested that the government fears it may remain above 2.5m for the rest of the decade. The human cost is evident, not least in the growing preponderance of the long-term unemployed: more than 53% of the unemployed have now been without a job for over six months and about 31% have not worked for more than a year. (The comparative figures a year ago were 44% and 25%.) And the financial cost to the taxpayer, if less emotive, is hardly less sobering: basic social-security payments to the unemployed will cost some £7.6 billion ($14.1 billion) this year.

Few people at Westminster retain much faith in remedies at a macroeconomic level. As the chancellor, Norman Lamont, underlined again in a speech to an audience of businessmen this week, economic policy remains firmly fixed on other goals – the fight against inflation, the need to sustain sterling within the exchange-rate mechanism – leaving unemployment to rise or fall as a consequence. But the corollary should be a more lively concern with the microeconomics of unemployment and the experience of those dealing with it every day.

Talk to the jobless in Tower Hamlets, a London borough covering a swathe of London's east end, where 20% of the workforce is unemployed, and one complaint is heard above all others: the jobs on offer in local job centres are not worth taking, because they do not pay enough. Anyone taking a job loses not only his dole money but also housing benefit, which automatically covers all his rent. Many prefer to remain unemployed, grabbing the occasional chance to earn extra cash in the black economy.

The poverty traps set by welfare-payment thresholds have been a concern for years, and the government has tried to lessen their impact. For example, those who take a low-wage job in place of the dole can now claim 'family credit', if they have children to support. And the pre-election budget reduced the lower-rate tax-band from 25p to 20p in the pound for the first £2,000 of earnings. But few expect such measures to have much impact. Frank Field, a Labour MP whose views on the welfare state are widely respected at Westminster, has no doubt that something deeper than benefit traps is holding back many of the unemployed: the growing distance between them and the traditional work ethic. *For many young people, in particular, unemployment is becoming a habit that is hard to kick.*

Short of pushing benefits down below subsistence levels, how can the system be redesigned to drive the reluctant back to work? Mr Field would start by getting unemployed young men (in his experience, men are the worst offenders) to turn up at the job centre more regularly than once a fortnight – the current rule. More radical would be either (a) to introduce what Americans call 'workfare' where, in some states, welfare payments are halted if claimants refuse a job offer; or (b) to limit the length of time an unemployed person can remain on welfare (presently unlimited).

But go back to the jobless in Tower Hamlets: they have other problems, too. Employers increasingly require work experience, even for the most menial of jobs. The government claims to have met this need with a new work-experience scheme, Employment Action; but it has only 61,000 places. Critics say it does not always offer useful experience: one Tower Hamlets man had been delivering meals to old ladies but was looking for a job in construction. Most fundamental of all, the unemployed are too often lacking in basic skills – not just to do a decent job, but even to apply for one.

Here the job centres could surely do more, if they had more resources. The average job adviser in Britain copes with five times as many cases in a week as his counterpart in Sweden; the unemployed, as a result, get little consistent and personalised help from the service. If John Major is serious about 'empowering' those who are dependent on public services, as he claimed this week in a speech to the Adam Smith Institute, then the job centres would be as good a place to start as any.

Source: *Economist,* 20 June 1992.

I hear that this ELECTION is about INCOME TAX...

JOB CENTRE

calum

To rely on the movement in unemployment as the prime indicator ignores the damage that a high level of unemployment brings in its wake. Unemployment can remain neglected in many quarters because its effects remain unseen. It drives people into their homes. It destroys marriages and impairs health. It stops the will to struggle. Only occasionally does the public see the appalling damage it does. The public notice unemployment when it is increasing rapidly (it might be their own jobs that are on the line) or when the unemployed march to protest against the lack of work. But it is easy to forget.

Yet the fight against unemployment is as much in the interest of the employed as the unemployed. Unemployment benefits and the consequent loss of taxes cost the employed roughly £25 billion, or £1000 per worker. Thus unemployment is like an invisible drain in a pond. It lowers the level for everyone. If we tackle unemployment, we shall all gain.

But can it be done? This brings us to our last objection.

Objection 3: Full employment is impossible, so we should adjust to unemployment

According to this view, the main need is to fund creative uses of time for people who do not have paid work. However, our previous argument shows that there are economic gains to be made from putting the unemployed back to work. There are equity gains, as most unemployed people want a paid job in order to avoid feeling disadvantaged, and there are efficiency gains, as national output is lower if we let a valuable resource go to waste.

Society owes its members the chance of paid work. And we *can*, given the will, provide enough jobs. Other countries like Sweden do, and Britain did so for most of the post-war period. If this objection prevails future historians will look back on the 1980s and early 1990s, as on the 1930s, and marvel at how quickly people assumed that a temporary aberration was permanent.

We could move steadily back towards full employment, if we thought it mattered sufficiently. But do we?

```
┌─────────────────────────────────────────────────────────────┐
│                        KEY WORDS                            │
│                                                             │
│  Wage inflation               Government debt               │
│  Balance of payments          Unemployment level            │
│  Real interest rates          Full employment               │
│  Public sector borrowing requirement   1930s                │
└─────────────────────────────────────────────────────────────┘
```

Reading list
Layard, R. and Philpott, J., *Stopping Unemployment*, Employment Institute, 1991.

Essay topics
1 Compare the relative costs of unemployment and inflation to the economy. Discuss whether or not it is possible to reduce unemployment without increasing inflation. (Joint Matriculation Board, 1992)
2 (a) How, in principle, can government use fiscal policy to influence the level of unemployment? (b) What arguments have been advanced against the use of government policy of this sort? (Welsh Joint Education Committee, 1990)
3 'British membership of the European exchange rate mechanism is a strategy designed to reduce the rate of inflation at the expense of domestic output and employment.' Discuss. (Oxford and Cambridge Schools Examination Board, 1991)
4 Evaluate different economic explanations of the current level of unemployment in the United Kingdom. (Associated Examining Board, 1992)
5 To what extent is unemployment the result of real wages being too high? (University of Oxford Delegacy of Local Examinations, 1991)

Data Response Question 7

The saving ratio
This task is based on a question set by the Oxford and Cambridge Schools Examination Board in 1992. Read the article, which is adapted from the Bank of England's *Quarterly Bulletin* (May 1991) and *UK Economics Analyst* (July/August 1991), and answer the following questions.

1 Define (i) saving ratio; (ii) income gearing; (iii) deregulation; (iv) real personal disposable income.

2 Why is there 'considerable uncertainty' about the behaviour of the saving ratio in 1991/92?

3 Explain 'the need to correct part of the build up of consumer and corporate debt'.

4 Explain why 'because of ERM constraints, real interest rates are likely to remain higher than usual during a recovery phase'.

5 What is a 'balance of payments constraint', and why might it 'intervene to prevent growth from running at the normal 2–2.5% rate'?

6 Why, despite recovery, is unemployment likely to continue to rise?

The strength of the recovery

The period since mid-1988 has seen a sharp recovery in the *saving ratio* as consumption growth has slowed. The ratio reached 10.8% in the fourth quarter of 1990. The sharp reduction in the mid-1980s coincided with a rapid expansion of personal borrowing and a rise in *income gearing*, resulting in part from *deregulation* and competition in financial services. It also reflected the restoration of consumer confidence in the wake of strong and sustained growth of *real personal disposable income* and a marked improvement in job security. There is *considerable uncertainty* this time as to whether the response of the personal sector to rising real incomes will be to allow the saving ratio to fall again. On the other hand, there is evidence that saving rises to restore the real value of wealth eroded by inflation, so as inflation falls, the need to save for this purpose is reduced.

The likelihood is that the saving ratio will remain high for several more quarters because of the impact of rising unemployment. There are other reasons for believing that the early stages of economic recovery will be slow. These include *the need to correct part of the build up of consumer and corporate debt* which occurred during the boom; the likelihood that the German economy will weaken substantially in 1992, keeping European growth well below trend; and the fact that, *because of ERM constraints, real interest rates are likely to remain higher than usual during a recovery phase*. Taken together, these factors suggest that the first 12–18 months of the recovery will see growth at about 1.5% p.a. A *balance of payments constraint* might later intervene to prevent growth from running at the normal 2–2.5% rate. Even this would not be enough to reduce the level of unemployment following its likely rise to almost 3 millions in 1992.

Conclusion

Unemployment has been the biggest single economic problem in the UK since the 1970s but governments have not regarded it as such. In the 1980s, and now again in the early 1990s, disinflation is the overriding priority, and the unemployment that it produces is regarded as a nasty, but necessary, side-effect of the battle against inflation. Unemployment shows no sign of disappearing of its own accord, nor have government policies averted persistent levels of unemployment that would have been unthinkable twenty years ago.

We have shown in Chapter 2 that unemployment is intrinsically linked to inflation via the behaviour of firms and unions. This is such that if unemployment is above the NAIRU inflation falls, and if unemployment is below the NAIRU inflation rises. This relationship explains why policies that have reduced unemployment without changing the NAIRU have been inflationary. It also explains why anti-inflationary policies require increasing unemployment. In order to be able to lower unemployment without causing inflation, or reduce inflation without increasing unemployment, we must reduce the NAIRU. In this context Chapter 6 discussed a number of policies designed to put more people in work without sparking off inflation; for example by concentrating resources on the large number of long-term unemployed and via education and training for all workers. One can argue about whether the current level of unemployment really is a price worth paying to beat inflation, but in any case the non-inflationary reduction of unemployment is surely preferable to policies involving such a trade-off.

A recent evaluation of the economy (by Layard and Nickell) suggested that 'the ultimate criteria for economic policy are productivity, unemployment, inflation and income distribution'. A cut in the NAIRU allows lower unemployment and inflation, improves the distribution of income by putting more of the labour force in employment, and can be associated with greater productivity if achieved through training.

The relevance of policies to reduce unemployment cannot easily be exaggerated. At the time of writing, unemployment on the claimant count definition stands at 2.8 million (10.1 per cent) and job losses are running at a rate of 8000 per week, more than twice the rate of the blackest times in the 1980s (see Figure 25). There is no sign of any improvement in unemployment; indeed, most predictions are for

Tuesday, 29 September	
Defence Research Agency: Portsmouth and across South	1950
Sears Group: 350 shoe shops to close across UK	1800
Northern Telecom: Belfast, Basildon and Wales	400
Pirelli Cables: Eastleigh and Newport	300
ITN: mainly in London	112
Tullis Russell: Fife paper factory	37
RAF Saxa Vord: Unst in Shetland	30
Wednesday, 30 September	
IBM: 26 sites across UK	600
Essex County Council: Chelmsford	440
Boulton & Paul: 18 sites inc Norwich, Maldon, Lowestoft	387
BBC: Pebble Mill and London	129
Powergen: various sites	120
Research Machines: Oxford computer firm	120
National Power: Agecroft plant in Manchester	100
Marine Products: Southampton shipbuilders	100
Eastern Electricity: Ipswich	90
Trainload Freight: Grangemouth, Scotland	90
Sunblest Bakeries: Bradford, West Yorkshire	65
Yardley Lentheric: Basildon, Essex	50
Thursday, 1 October	
British Nuclear Fuels: Sellafield	1000
Cadbury Schweppes: mainly in Birmingham	450
VSEL submarine shipyard: Barrow-in-Furness, Cumbria	390
Construction Industry Training Board: across country	156
3i Group: Brighton, Guildford, Milton Keynes, Sheffield	100
Friday, 2 October	
Dowty Aerospace: Staverton and Wolverhampton	265
Vosper Thornycroft: Southampton shipbuilders	200
Liverpool Broadgreen Hospital: cleaning jobs	180
Birds Eye Walls: Gloucester ice-cream factory	40
Weekly total	**9701**

Figure 25 Reported job losses in one week in 1992

further rises. Nor, on current government policies, does there appear to be much hope of a reversal in the future. The current level of unemployment is estimated to cost the taxpayer £25 billion per year. Adding to this figure the human cost from several million frustrated workers, their families and friends, it is hard to believe that there are no worthwhile alternatives. The experience of other countries has shown us that no country need suffer high unemployment permanently, and the analysis contained in this book has demonstrated that *it is within the government's power to influence the level of unemployment.*

Index